# Exploring the Rainforest

HERE'S TO LOTS +
LOTS OF EXCITING
DISCOVERIES.

Exploring the Rainforest

Science Activities for Kids

Anthony D. Fredericks

Illustrated by Shawn Berlute-Shea

FULCRUM PUBLISHING
GOLDEN, COLORADO

To Barbara—

for writing inspiration.

Library of Congress Cataloging-in-Publication Data

Fredericks, Anthony D.
  Exploring the rainforest : science activities for kids / Anthony D. Fredericks
   p. cm.
  Includes bibliographical references and index.
  Summary: Provides instructions for activities that explore the ecosystem of the tropical rainforest.
  ISBN 1-55591-304-0 (pbk.)
  1. Rainforest ecology—Study and teaching—Activity programs—Juvenile literature. 2. Rainforests—Study and teaching—Activity programs—Juvenile literature. 3. Rainforest ecology—Experiments—Juvenile literature. 4. Rainforests—Experiments—Juvenile literature. [1. Rainforests—Experiments. 2. Rainforest ecology—Experiments. 3. Ecology—Experiments. 4. Experiments.]
  I. Title.
  QH541.5.R27F74   1996
  574.5'2642—dc20   96-4963
                     CIP
                       AC

 Text printed on recycled paper

Printed in the United States of America

0 9 8 7 6 5 4 3 2 1

Fulcrum Publishing
350 Indiana Street, Suite 350
Golden, Colorado 80401-5093
(800) 992-2908 • (303) 277-1623

Contents

Acknowledgments

The author is indebted to Hugo Llamas, the Information Coordinator at the Rainforest Action Network, for providing pertinent data and invaluable resources during the research for this book. The RAN is a testament to the positive possibilities of people working together for environmental protection.

Introduction

Along ribbon of 20 million army ants moves silently over a thick blanket of leaves. Liana vines—up to 3,000 feet long—drape themselves from the tops of the tallest trees. A snake releases its grip on a spiraling tree branch and "flies" through the air to land on the trunk of a kapok tree. A frog with skin so poisonous it can kill a human swims in a small pool of water inside a colorful flower. Dozens of plants without roots or soil thrive high above the forest floor. A hairy tarantula pounces on an unsuspecting bird, plunging its fangs deep into the bird's body. This is the rainforest—magical, mysterious and full of wonder. It is an assembly of plants and animals woven together through a complex web of life and death in an environment unlike any other.

The rainforest is a place overflowing with more plants and animals than any other spot on earth … a place that covers less than 10 percent of the earth's surface, yet contains over 60 percent of all the plant and animal species ever discovered … a place where more than 1,600 varieties of vegetables grow, trees soar more than 200 feet into the air and a 35-pound flower grows. It's also a place where strange green animals travel upside down through the trees, where lizards parachute through the air and where armies of termites eat tons of wood every year!

The rainforest is a magical place to explore—there's a new discovery around every bend and high in every tree. Shimmering blue butterflies, monkeys that fly, flowers with "landing pads" for insects and birds that can locate beehives are just some of the marvels that can be found in this incredible environment. But this is also an environment in danger! This marvelous place we call the rainforest is being destroyed at the rate of one football field every second. That's 1 million acres of trees lost every week. It's a place being burned to the ground by fires so large they can be seen from space shuttles as they orbit the earth. It's a place where the plant and animal species are being eliminated at the rate of one every hour—more than 20 species become extinct every day—never to return. Some scientists believe that in the next few decades the rainforests of the world will be totally wiped out. How and why this is happening will be explained in the pages ahead. More important, however, will be the active role you take in learning about the mysteries of the rainforest and what can be done to prevent its destruction.

This book is designed to provide you with exciting and fascinating information about the rainforest. It offers a number of hands-on activities and projects to help you learn about various aspects of this fragile ecosystem. You'll learn how to build a miniature rainforest in your bedroom; you'll learn how to use recipes with foods from the rainforest; you'll build a feeder to attract birds and you'll conduct plant experiments using the same type of soil found on the floor of the rainforest. I invite you to tackle as many of these projects as you wish; of course, the more you attempt, the more opportunities you will have to learn about the rainforest and all its mysteries. Each of the activities in this book has been designed to provide you with valuable learning experiences so that you might appreciate and work for the preservation of this important piece of our world.

I hope you enjoy these activities and that you will use them as stepping stones in learning more about this important ecosystem. The rainforest is a special place, and we need to work together to preserve what is left of the rainforest so that it can continue to be a lasting part of the planet Earth.

How to Use This Book

This is a book full of discoveries and full of wonder—a book where you'll finds lots to do and lots to explore. Here you'll get firsthand experiences in learning about and appreciating various elements of the rainforest. There are projects you can do indoors, discoveries you can make in your own backyard and "stuff" to learn everywhere you go. This book not only will *tell* you about parts of the rainforest, it also will *show* you what the rainforest is all about. You won't need a lot of equipment or expensive supplies—there are loads of rainforest activities, projects and discoveries for everyone within the pages of this book.

Throughout this book you'll see several symbols such as those below. These symbols identify an activity or project for you to try.

This symbol stands for an *activity*. The activities in this book are designed to help you appreciate selected portions of the rainforest and participate in real hands-on learning experiences.

This is a *look for it project*—something you can do in your own backyard, the playground, the area around your school or in your community. Look for it projects will help you compare parts of your local environment with the rainforest environment.

It is not necessary to complete every investigation in this book. You should feel free to select those activities with which you are most comfortable or in which you are most interested. I hope you enjoy your journey through this magical place called the rainforest.

Welcome to the Rainforest

It's amazing! It's fantastic! It's incredible! It's filled with flying snakes, poisonous frogs, flowers without stems and trees that strangle—an incredible conglomeration of plants and animals found nowhere else in the world. It's splashed with colors, saturated with dense and heavy air and pulsing with life. It's filled with a symphony of sounds and the eerie stillness of a haunted castle. It slithers, it crawls, it pounces and it attacks with claws, fangs and deadly juices. It's both life and death for hundreds of thousands of organisms every day; it's their home and their burial ground; it's their sustenance and their extermination. What is it? It's the rainforest, a magical, mysterious place that covers 6 percent of the earth's surface, yet is the sole environment for nearly 60 percent of the world's plant and animal species … so many that more than half of them have not even been discovered yet!

The Rainforest Checklist

▲ The average temperature does not vary by more than 15° throughout the entire year. The typical range of temperature may be as high as 90°F or as low as 75°F.

▲ It rains a lot—up to 400 inches a year.

▲ The average relative humidity ranges from 77 to 88 percent.

▲ The soil is nutrient poor, and usually not more than 1 or 2 inches deep.

▲ Most rainforests tend to be "clustered" around the equator.

▲ Rainforests are found in three major areas: Central and South America, Central Africa, and Southeast Asia and Australia.

▲ Rainforests have a lush and diverse variety of plants and animals.

Before we begin our discoveries in and around the rainforest, you may wish to create your own rainforest at home. The following activity will help you do just that.

Living Laboratory

A terrarium is a miniature controlled environment containing plants and animals in an artificial situation that can closely imitate the natural living conditions of rainforest organisms. Carefully set up, a rainforest terrarium can endure for long periods of time and provide you with a close-up look of this "sample" of nature.

You'll need:

a glass container (An old aquarium purchased at a pet
   store or garage sale, a large pickle jar or even a
   2-liter soda bottle can be used.)
small pebbles or rocks
bits of charcoal (Wood charcoal from a fire or
   aquarium charcoal from a local pet store work
   equally well.)
soil or potting soil
plants, rocks, pieces of wood
   small land animals

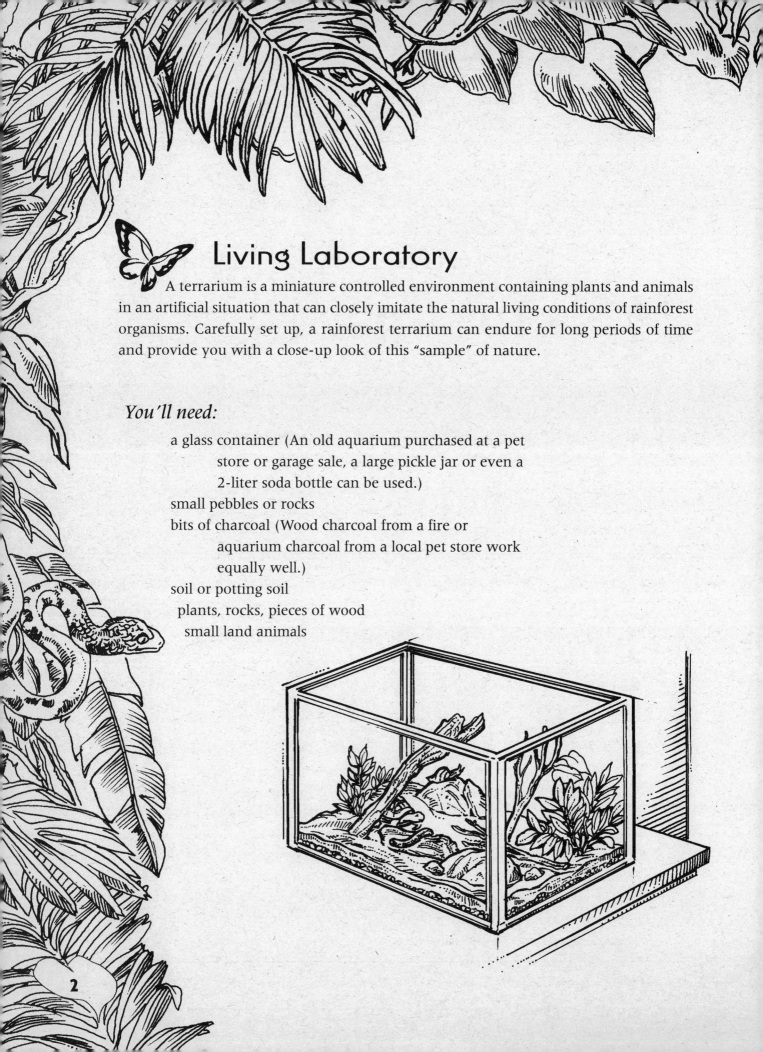

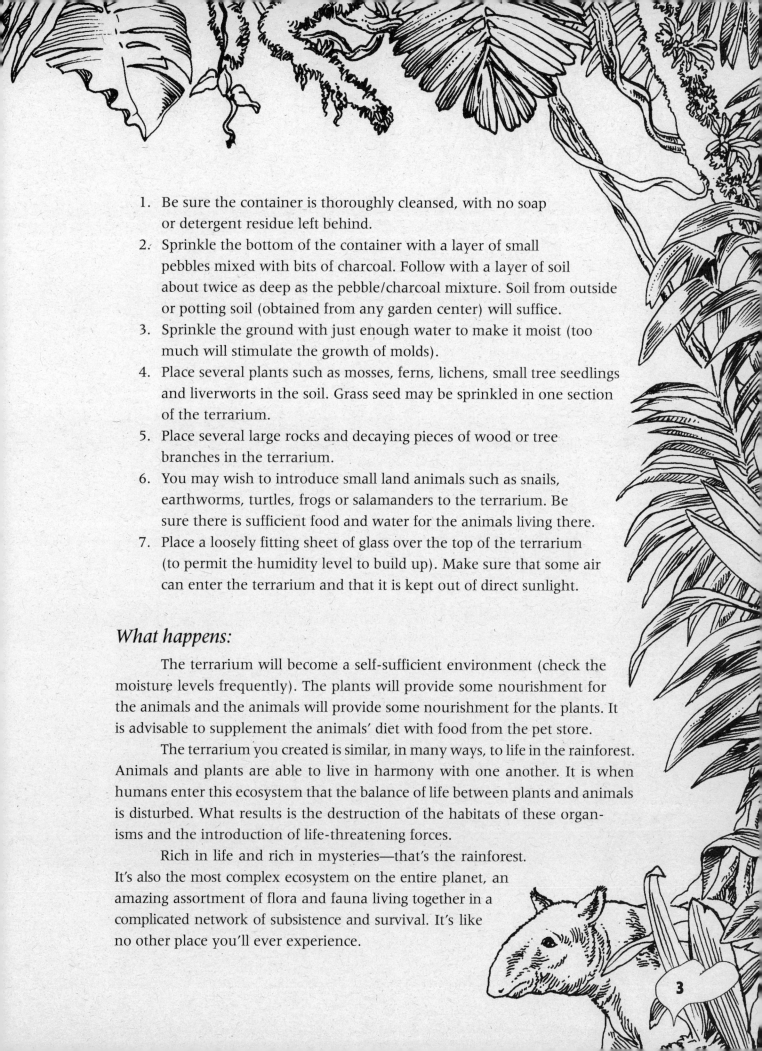

1. Be sure the container is thoroughly cleansed, with no soap or detergent residue left behind.

2. Sprinkle the bottom of the container with a layer of small pebbles mixed with bits of charcoal. Follow with a layer of soil about twice as deep as the pebble/charcoal mixture. Soil from outside or potting soil (obtained from any garden center) will suffice.

3. Sprinkle the ground with just enough water to make it moist (too much will stimulate the growth of molds).

4. Place several plants such as mosses, ferns, lichens, small tree seedlings and liverworts in the soil. Grass seed may be sprinkled in one section of the terrarium.

5. Place several large rocks and decaying pieces of wood or tree branches in the terrarium.

6. You may wish to introduce small land animals such as snails, earthworms, turtles, frogs or salamanders to the terrarium. Be sure there is sufficient food and water for the animals living there.

7. Place a loosely fitting sheet of glass over the top of the terrarium (to permit the humidity level to build up). Make sure that some air can enter the terrarium and that it is kept out of direct sunlight.

What happens:

The terrarium will become a self-sufficient environment (check the moisture levels frequently). The plants will provide some nourishment for the animals and the animals will provide some nourishment for the plants. It is advisable to supplement the animals' diet with food from the pet store.

The terrarium you created is similar, in many ways, to life in the rainforest. Animals and plants are able to live in harmony with one another. It is when humans enter this ecosystem that the balance of life between plants and animals is disturbed. What results is the destruction of the habitats of these organisms and the introduction of life-threatening forces.

Rich in life and rich in mysteries—that's the rainforest. It's also the most complex ecosystem on the entire planet, an amazing assortment of flora and fauna living together in a complicated network of subsistence and survival. It's like no other place you'll ever experience.

To help us appreciate the rainforest, let's take a walk through this amazing wonderland. Put on your hiking boots, zip up your waterproof jacket and grab your binoculars—we're about to make some incredible discoveries:

Look

A gold poison arrow frog casually rests along the edge of a bromeliad plant.

A half-mile-long column of army ants marches across the buttressed roots of an immense tree.

An algae-covered sloth carefully pulls its way through a clump of overhanging branches.

A alien-looking heliconid caterpillar pulls itself across the edge of a passionflower.

Listen

The whir of hummingbird wings makes a faint hum in the trees overhead.

A chirping green-headed tanager flits from branch to branch looking for some tasty insects to devour.

The shriek of a capuchin monkey echoes through the treetops as it escapes the claws of an approaching harpy eagle.

The flutter of the wings of fruit bats dances across the night sky.

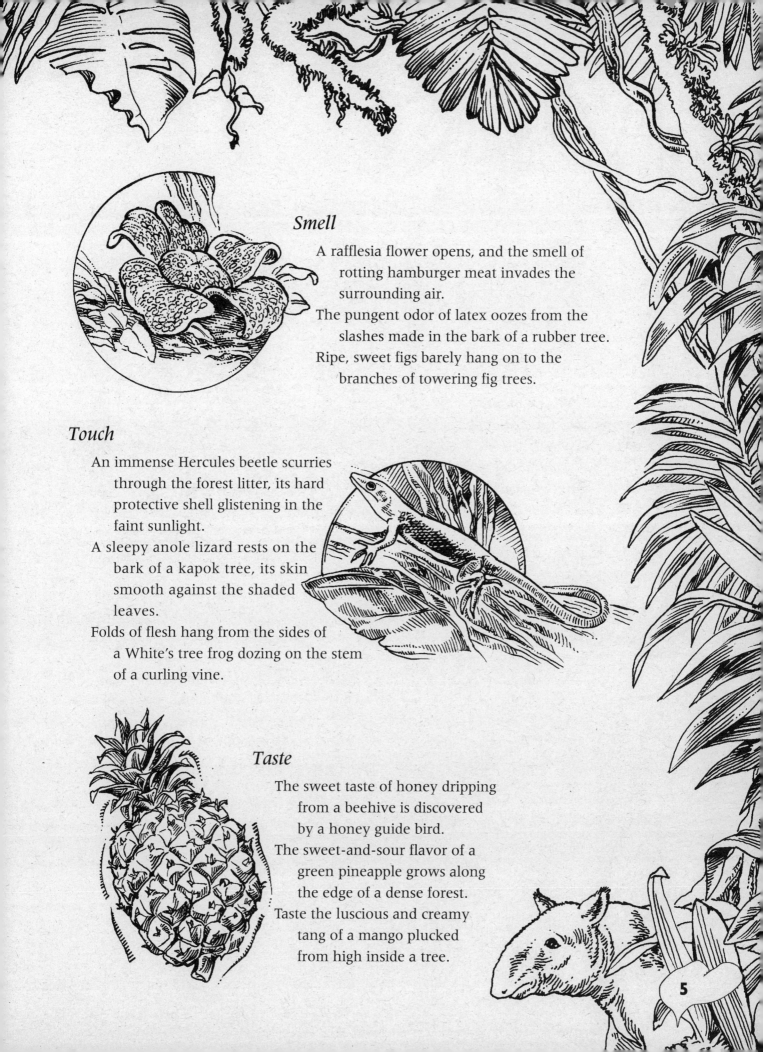

Smell

A rafflesia flower opens, and the smell of
rotting hamburger meat invades the
surrounding air.
The pungent odor of latex oozes from the
slashes made in the bark of a rubber tree.
Ripe, sweet figs barely hang on to the
branches of towering fig trees.

Touch

An immense Hercules beetle scurries
through the forest litter, its hard
protective shell glistening in the
faint sunlight.
A sleepy anole lizard rests on the
bark of a kapok tree, its skin
smooth against the shaded
leaves.
Folds of flesh hang from the sides of
a White's tree frog dozing on the stem
of a curling vine.

Taste

The sweet taste of honey dripping
from a beehive is discovered
by a honey guide bird.
The sweet-and-sour flavor of a
green pineapple grows along
the edge of a dense forest.
Taste the luscious and creamy
tang of a mango plucked
from high inside a tree.

5

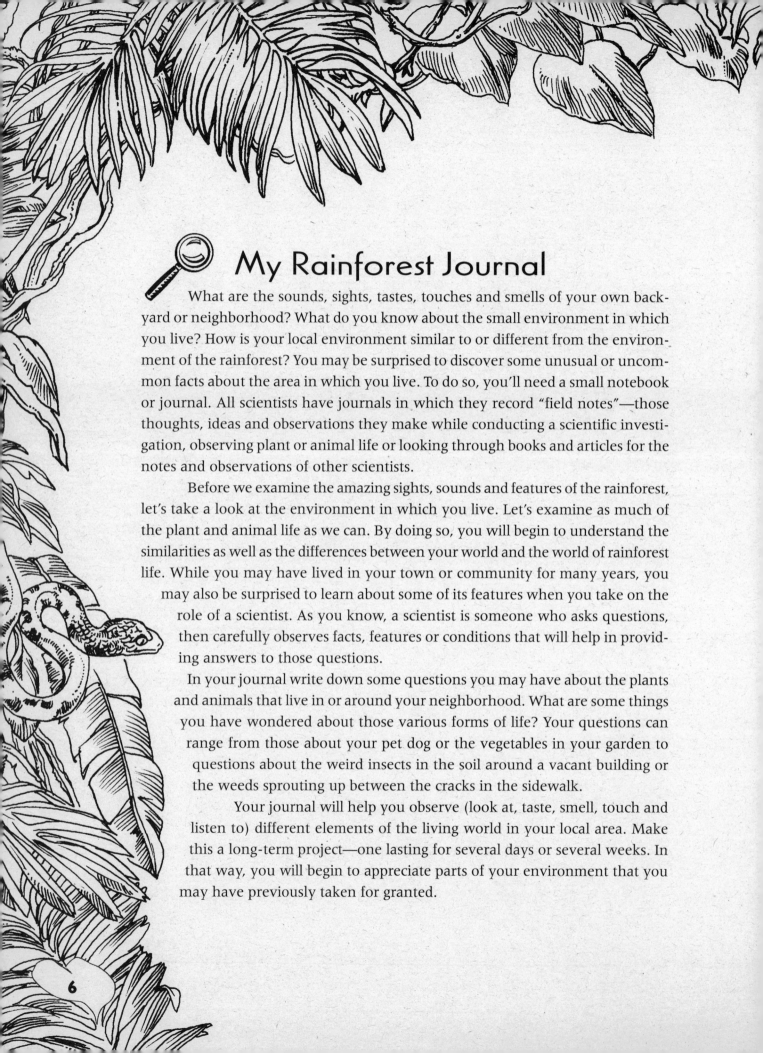

My Rainforest Journal

What are the sounds, sights, tastes, touches and smells of your own backyard or neighborhood? What do you know about the small environment in which you live? How is your local environment similar to or different from the environment of the rainforest? You may be surprised to discover some unusual or uncommon facts about the area in which you live. To do so, you'll need a small notebook or journal. All scientists have journals in which they record "field notes"—those thoughts, ideas and observations they make while conducting a scientific investigation, observing plant or animal life or looking through books and articles for the notes and observations of other scientists.

Before we examine the amazing sights, sounds and features of the rainforest, let's take a look at the environment in which you live. Let's examine as much of the plant and animal life as we can. By doing so, you will begin to understand the similarities as well as the differences between your world and the world of rainforest life. While you may have lived in your town or community for many years, you may also be surprised to learn about some of its features when you take on the role of a scientist. As you know, a scientist is someone who asks questions, then carefully observes facts, features or conditions that will help in providing answers to those questions.

In your journal write down some questions you may have about the plants and animals that live in or around your neighborhood. What are some things you have wondered about those various forms of life? Your questions can range from those about your pet dog or the vegetables in your garden to questions about the weird insects in the soil around a vacant building or the weeds sprouting up between the cracks in the sidewalk.

Your journal will help you observe (look at, taste, smell, touch and listen to) different elements of the living world in your local area. Make this a long-term project—one lasting for several days or several weeks. In that way, you will begin to appreciate parts of your environment that you may have previously taken for granted.

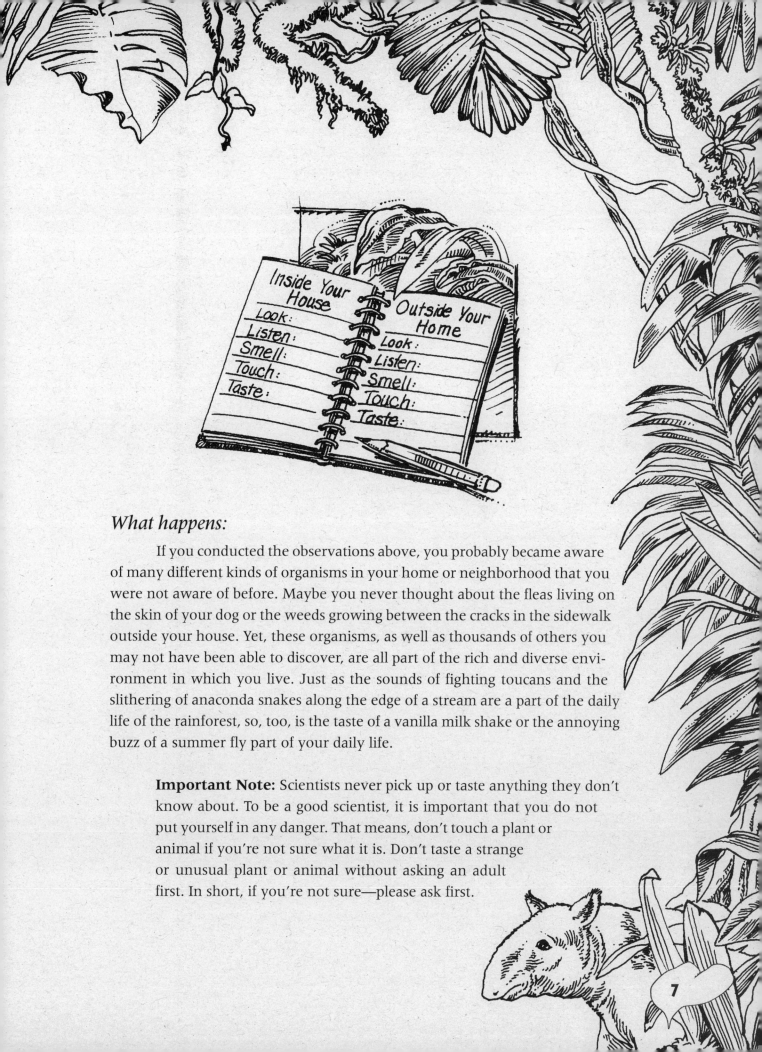

What happens:

If you conducted the observations above, you probably became aware of many different kinds of organisms in your home or neighborhood that you were not aware of before. Maybe you never thought about the fleas living on the skin of your dog or the weeds growing between the cracks in the sidewalk outside your house. Yet, these organisms, as well as thousands of others you may not have been able to discover, are all part of the rich and diverse environment in which you live. Just as the sounds of fighting toucans and the slithering of anaconda snakes along the edge of a stream are a part of the daily life of the rainforest, so, too, is the taste of a vanilla milk shake or the annoying buzz of a summer fly part of your daily life.

Important Note: Scientists never pick up or taste anything they don't know about. To be a good scientist, it is important that you do not put yourself in any danger. That means, don't touch a plant or animal if you're not sure what it is. Don't taste a strange or unusual plant or animal without asking an adult first. In short, if you're not sure—please ask first.

Pencil Park

Here's another activity that will help you appreciate the enormous variety of life in your own neighborhood or community.

Go into your yard or a nearby park. Push 4 sharpened pencils into the soil in a square pattern that is 1 foot on each side. Tie a piece of string around the 4 pencils so they form a miniature "boxing ring" on the ground. Lie down on your stomach and observe the variety of plant and animal life inside the square. You may wish to record all the different types of plants as well as the varieties of animal life and their habits as they creep, crawl or walk through the square. Visit your square at regular times throughout a period of several weeks. Be sure to observe and record all the life you see. You will undoubtedly discover a wide variety of plant and animal life in the square. In fact, you will probably be amazed at the many different forms of life found in just such a small space.

If you complete this activity over an extended period of time, you will notice how your miniature "environment" changes depending on the time of day, time of the year or varied weather patterns in your area. Changes in the rainforest are less dramatic, but no less surprising.

We'll be looking at many different elements of the rainforest through-out this book. I invite you to observe the varied elements of your own immediate environment, too. By comparing the sights and sounds of the rainforest with the sights and sounds of your own part of the country, you may begin to appreciate all the aspects and dimensions of this magical wonderland we call the rainforest.

8

Rain, Rain, All the Day

The rainforest is called a rainforest for one very simple reason—lots and lots of rain. The average rainforest gets about 80 inches of rain a year, while a few rainforests in the world get as much as 400 inches. That's 20 to 40 times more rain than Los Angeles gets in one year!

Most of the world's rainforests are located in a "belt" around the middle of the earth. This belt sits on both sides of the equator and stretches from the Tropic of Capricorn south of the equator to the Tropic of Cancer north of the equator. This portion of the earth is approximately the same distance from the sun throughout the year. As a result, the sun's rays strike this part of the earth almost directly; thus, the air is constantly warmed. Warm air is able to hold more moisture than cold air. When it rains, water collects on the plants, is heated by the warm air, evaporates from the plants, rises from the forest and cools. Clouds are formed filled with this moisture and it begins to rain again. This seemingly endless cycle is also supplemented by winds blowing in off the Atlantic Ocean bringing more moisture.

Raindrops Keep Falling . . .

This activity will help you measure the amount of rain that falls in your part of the world. The instrument you create will help you accumulate rainfall data over an extended period of time—a week, a month, a year.

You'll need:

    a tall jar (An olive jar works best.)
    a ruler
    a felt-tip pen
    a funnel

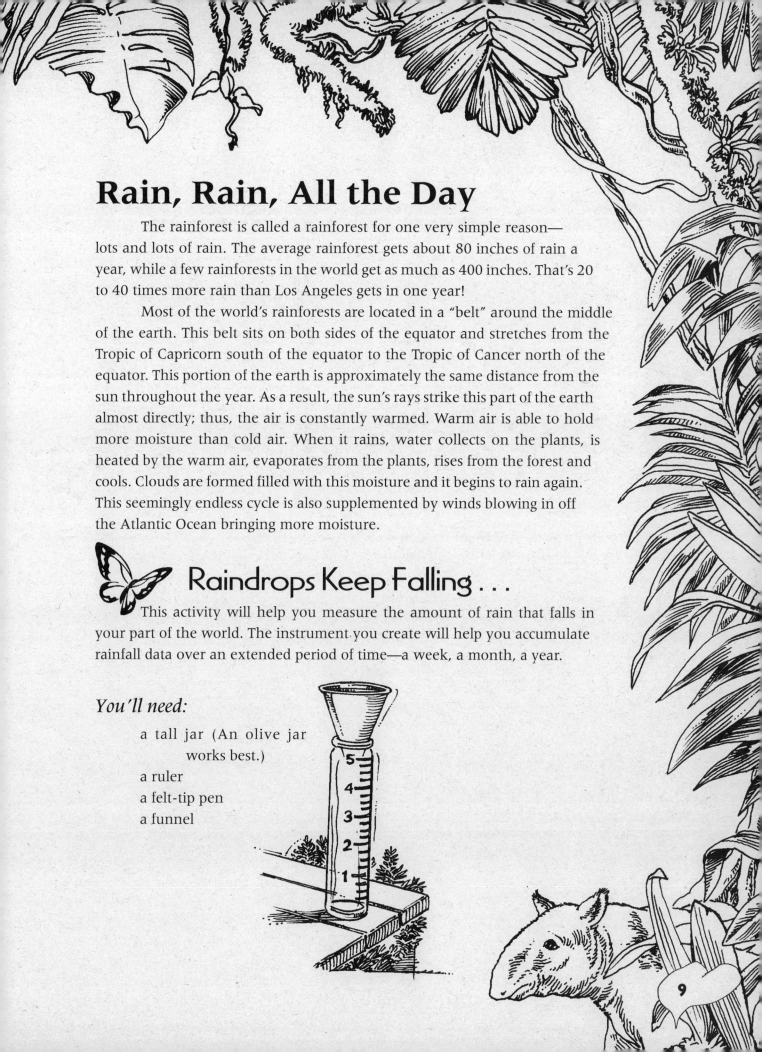

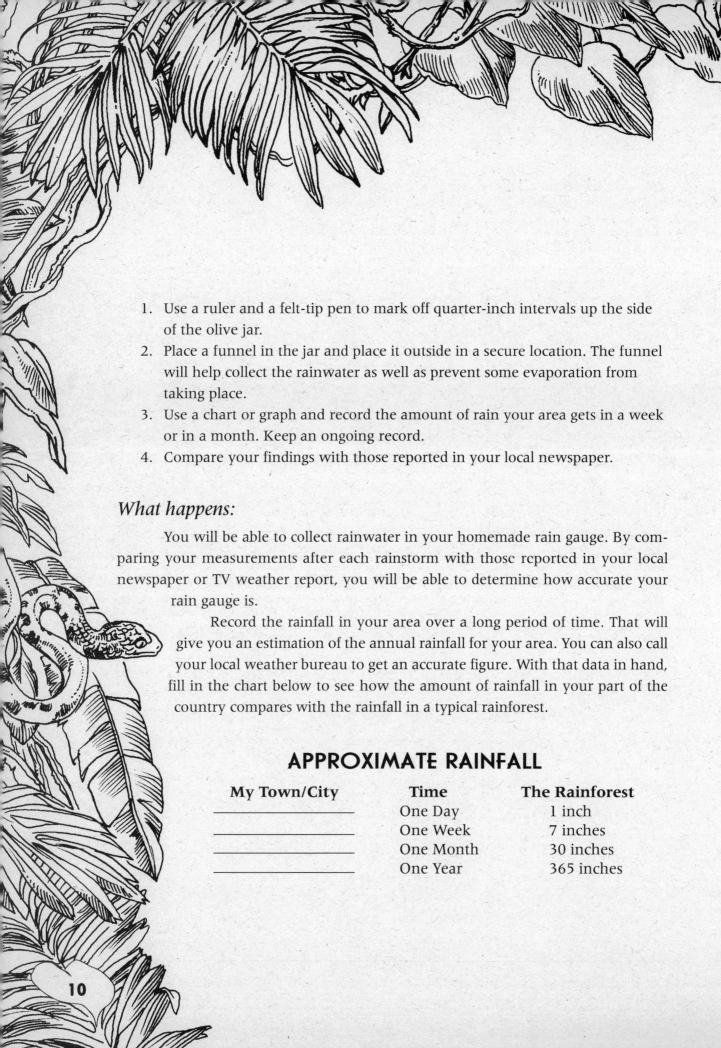

1. Use a ruler and a felt-tip pen to mark off quarter-inch intervals up the side of the olive jar.
2. Place a funnel in the jar and place it outside in a secure location. The funnel will help collect the rainwater as well as prevent some evaporation from taking place.
3. Use a chart or graph and record the amount of rain your area gets in a week or in a month. Keep an ongoing record.
4. Compare your findings with those reported in your local newspaper.

What happens:

You will be able to collect rainwater in your homemade rain gauge. By comparing your measurements after each rainstorm with those reported in your local newspaper or TV weather report, you will be able to determine how accurate your rain gauge is.

Record the rainfall in your area over a long period of time. That will give you an estimation of the annual rainfall for your area. You can also call your local weather bureau to get an accurate figure. With that data in hand, fill in the chart below to see how the amount of rainfall in your part of the country compares with the rainfall in a typical rainforest.

APPROXIMATE RAINFALL

My Town/City	Time	The Rainforest
_____	One Day	1 inch
_____	One Week	7 inches
_____	One Month	30 inches
_____	One Year	365 inches

The Web of Life

Different organisms get their food in different ways. Some organisms, known as *producers*, can manufacture their own food. Most plants are producers. However, most organisms cannot manufacture their own food and must consume food from another source; they are known as *consumers*. Most animals are consumers.

The plants and animals in a given environment are linked together through a series of feeding relationships. Plants use energy from the sun to produce food. This food is eaten by some animals, providing the energy they need to survive. These animals may then be eaten by other (usually larger) animals. In turn, those animals may be eaten by another group of (even larger) animals. This series of stages in which one organism is dependent on another organism for its survival (and so on) is known as a *food chain*. The following diagrams illustrate two different food chains.

As you look at the food chains above, you might expect that the consumption of one organism by another, which is in turn consumed by yet another organism, might happen in a straight line (see the illustration). However, nature is never quite that simple. Several organisms may be involved at several different levels, each dependent on *several others* for its food supply. This type of arrangement is known as a *food web*. Since most organisms eat more than one type of food, most organisms belong to more than one food chain. When several food chains are combined they form a food web. The following diagram illustrates one food web you might discover in the rainforest:

You will probably note that there are a number of food chains represented in the food web above. In short, there is a complex series of relationships that exists in the rainforest, relationships that help ensure the survival of the greatest number of plant and animal species. In other words, every plant and animal is dependent on every other plant and animal to live and survive.

Plants of the Rainforest

You might expect that in the wet, humid conditions of the rainforest, a host of plants would grow. That's true. In fact, there is probably a greater variety of plants in the rainforests of the world than there is in any other location. Here's a small sampling of specific plants you'll discover in the rainforest:

- orchids (There are more than 20,000 different species of orchids in the rainforest.)
- erythrine tree
- ferns
- mosses
- Brazil nut tree
- kapok tree (Fibers from the kapok tree are used in the manufacture of life preservers.)
- fig tree
- strangler fig (These trees grow up and around other trees, eventually cutting off their sunlight and food supplies. The host tree dies, leaving the strangler fig standing in its place.)
  - cecropia tree
  - philodendron
  - vanilla beans (used in the manufacture of vanilla, a popular flavoring)
  - passionflowers
  - cannonball tree (Its fruits are shaped exactly like cannonballs and frequently fall to the forest floor with loud crashes.)
  - Swiss cheese plant
  - queen's wreath
  - palm trees
  - pitcher plants (These are carnivorous plants—plants that eat small insects and other animals that fall into their open "mouths.")

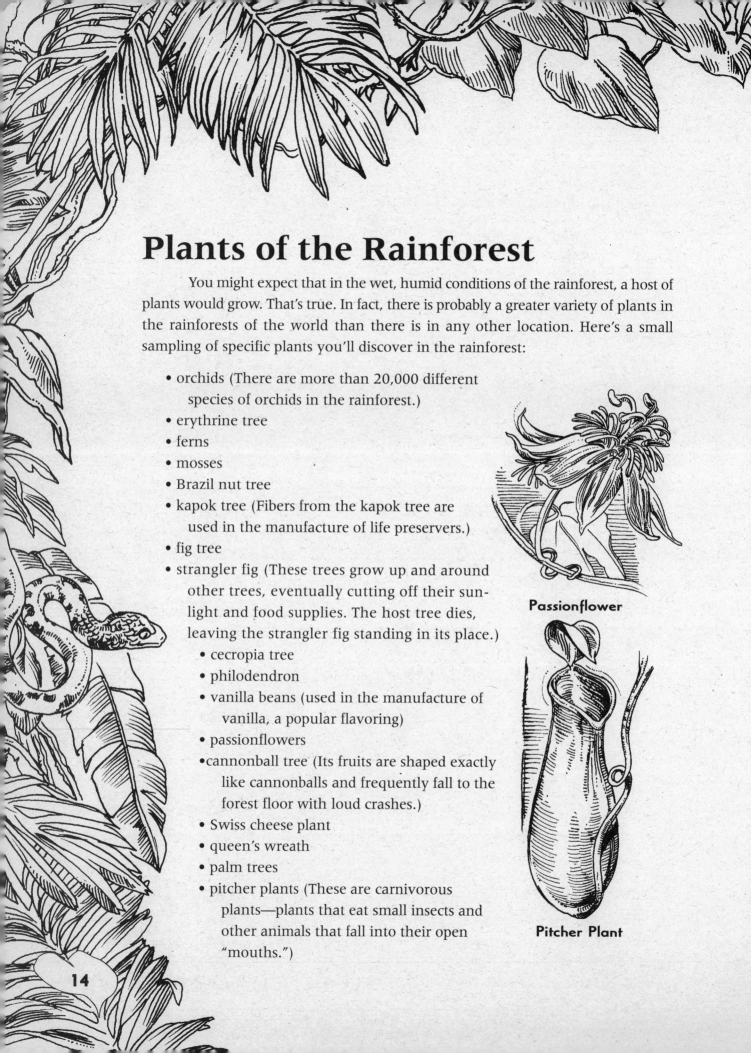

Passionflower

Pitcher Plant

Growing Up

If you want to grow some rainforest plants in your own home, visit a large supermarket, garden shop or nursery and look for one or more of the following rainforest plants:

African violet	begonia
bird's-nest fern	bromeliad
Christmas cactus	corn plant
croton	dumb cane
fiddle-leaf fig	orchid
philodendron	prayer plant
rubber plant	snake plant
umbrella tree	zebra plant

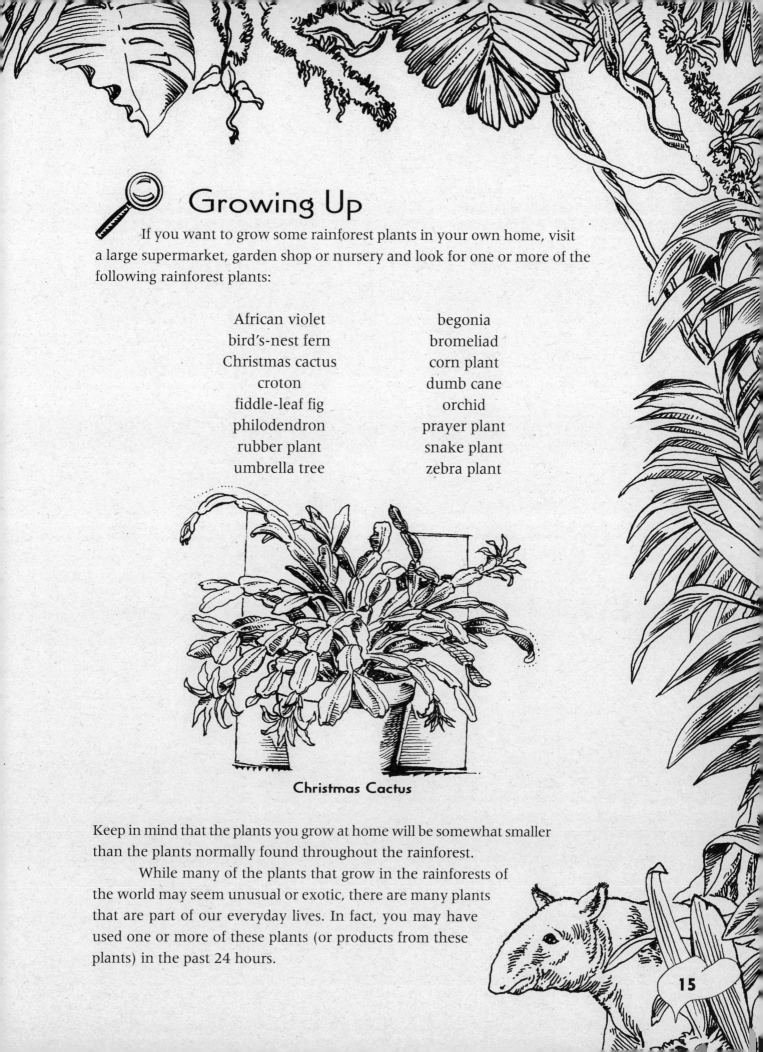

Christmas Cactus

Keep in mind that the plants you grow at home will be somewhat smaller than the plants normally found throughout the rainforest.

While many of the plants that grow in the rainforests of the world may seem unusual or exotic, there are many plants that are part of our everyday lives. In fact, you may have used one or more of these plants (or products from these plants) in the past 24 hours.

Animals of the Rainforest

A small, brightly colored bird rests on a tree branch high above the forest floor. Nearby, a silent and deadly killer patiently waits. Slowly the attacker approaches the bird, with no sound and just the barest of movement to give it away. The bird doesn't notice the approaching doom. The killer inches closer and closer until suddenly it pounces on the hapless victim, sinking its fangs deep into the flesh of the bird. Poison is injected into the bird's body and it quickly dies—becoming a tasty meal for the ferocious killer.

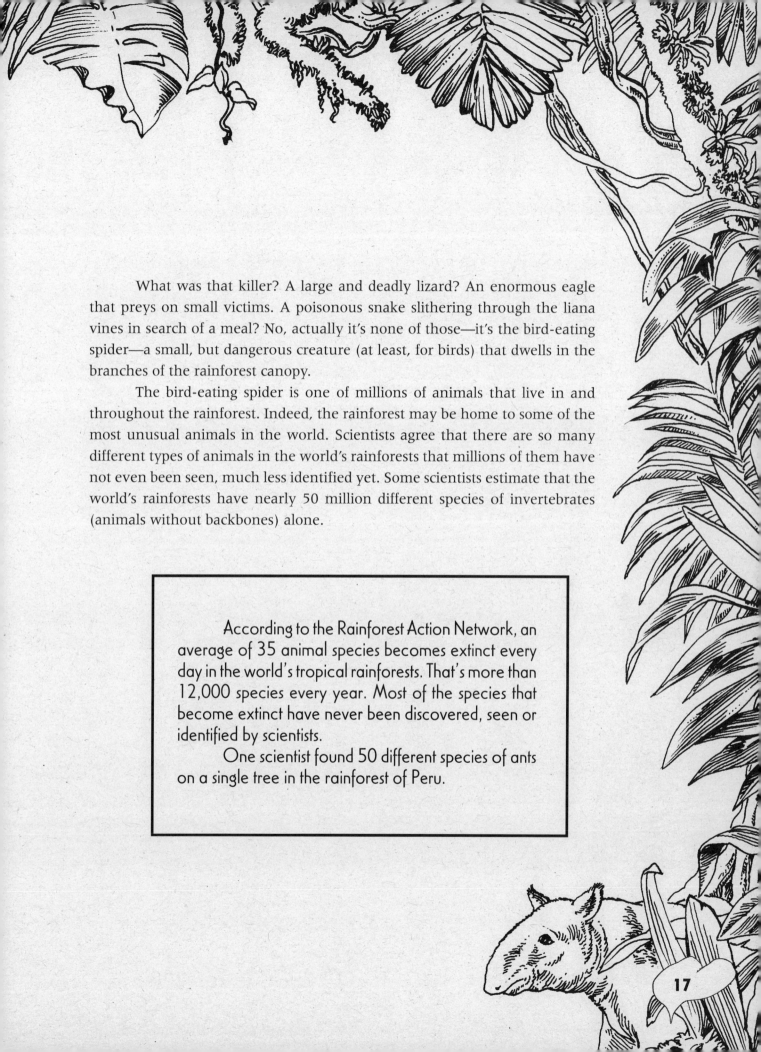

What was that killer? A large and deadly lizard? An enormous eagle that preys on small victims. A poisonous snake slithering through the liana vines in search of a meal? No, actually it's none of those—it's the bird-eating spider—a small, but dangerous creature (at least, for birds) that dwells in the branches of the rainforest canopy.

The bird-eating spider is one of millions of animals that live in and throughout the rainforest. Indeed, the rainforest may be home to some of the most unusual animals in the world. Scientists agree that there are so many different types of animals in the world's rainforests that millions of them have not even been seen, much less identified yet. Some scientists estimate that the world's rainforests have nearly 50 million different species of invertebrates (animals without backbones) alone.

According to the Rainforest Action Network, an average of 35 animal species becomes extinct every day in the world's tropical rainforests. That's more than 12,000 species every year. Most of the species that become extinct have never been discovered, seen or identified by scientists.

One scientist found 50 different species of ants on a single tree in the rainforest of Peru.

The following list is a small sampling of the enormous variety of animals found in the world's rainforests:

alligator	amazon parrot
anaconda	anteater
armadillo	bird-eating spider
capybara	electric eel
emerald tree boa	giant otter
grasshopper	harpy eagle
hoatzin	hummingbird
iguana	jaguar
katydid	king vulture
kinkajou	leaf-cutter ant
macaw	marmoset
millipede	morpho butterfly
nightjar	ocelot
pit viper	poison arrow frog
praying mantis	quetzal
sloth	spider monkey
squirrel monkey	tamandua
tanager	tapir
tent-making bat	toucan
tree frog	tree porcupine
wasp	white-tailed deer

Hoatzin

Jaguar

Surviving in the Rainforest

As you might imagine, with all the animals competing for food and space, survival is a top priority. Capturing one's own food and avoiding becoming food for another animal is a constant and daily struggle. In short, there is a great deal of competition that takes place throughout the rainforest.

Adaptation

One way animals have learned how to survive is through a process known as adaptation. This process means that animals have "learned" how to live in a specific environment and use the resources that are available in that environment. In other words, organisms develop features or behaviors that help them survive in a particular place over a period of years (usually hundreds or thousands of years). For example, toucans, with their enormous bills, have adapted to rainforest life because they can use those bills to break open the fruits that are a mainstay of their diet. The rainforest is filled with a variety of fruits that are accessible by toucans and other large-billed birds.

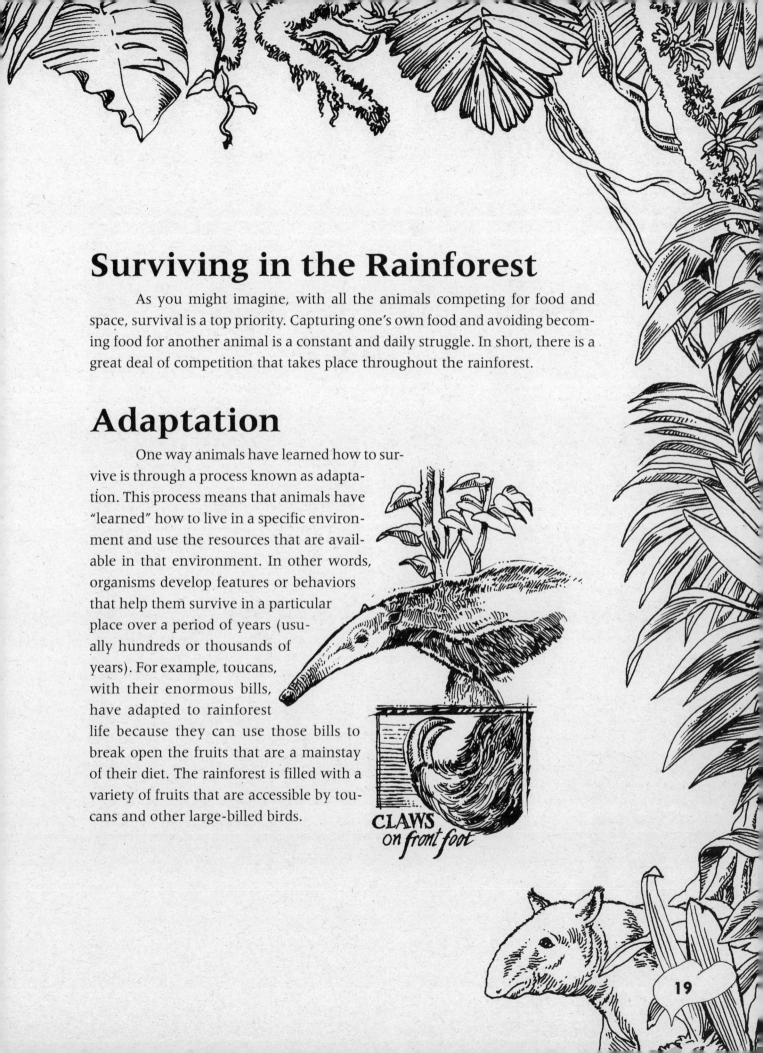

CLAWS
on front foot

19

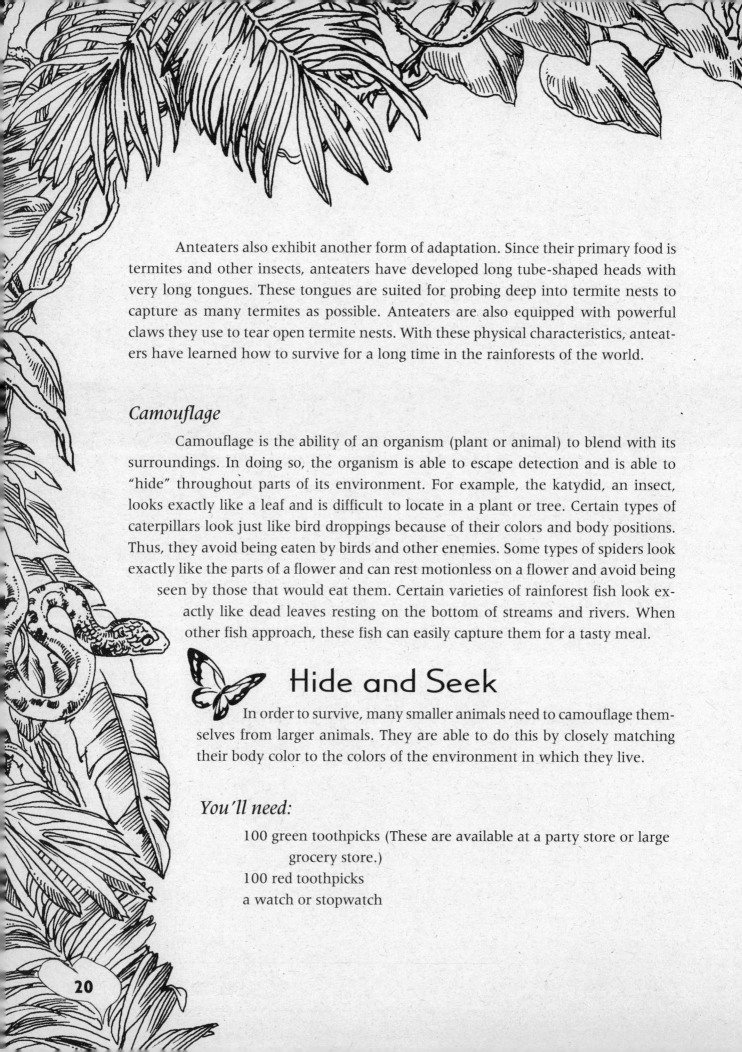

Anteaters also exhibit another form of adaptation. Since their primary food is termites and other insects, anteaters have developed long tube-shaped heads with very long tongues. These tongues are suited for probing deep into termite nests to capture as many termites as possible. Anteaters are also equipped with powerful claws they use to tear open termite nests. With these physical characteristics, anteaters have learned how to survive for a long time in the rainforests of the world.

Camouflage

Camouflage is the ability of an organism (plant or animal) to blend with its surroundings. In doing so, the organism is able to escape detection and is able to "hide" throughout parts of its environment. For example, the katydid, an insect, looks exactly like a leaf and is difficult to locate in a plant or tree. Certain types of caterpillars look just like bird droppings because of their colors and body positions. Thus, they avoid being eaten by birds and other enemies. Some types of spiders look exactly like the parts of a flower and can rest motionless on a flower and avoid being seen by those that would eat them. Certain varieties of rainforest fish look exactly like dead leaves resting on the bottom of streams and rivers. When other fish approach, these fish can easily capture them for a tasty meal.

Hide and Seek

In order to survive, many smaller animals need to camouflage themselves from larger animals. They are able to do this by closely matching their body color to the colors of the environment in which they live.

You'll need:

100 green toothpicks (These are available at a party store or large grocery store.)
100 red toothpicks
a watch or stopwatch

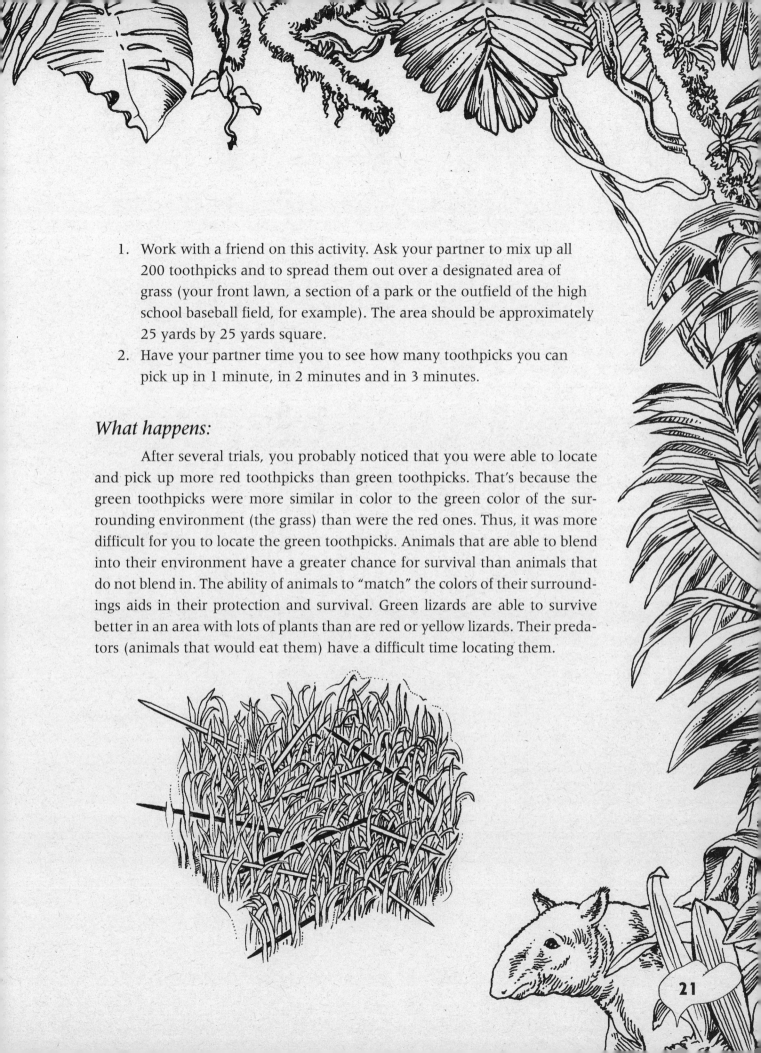

1. Work with a friend on this activity. Ask your partner to mix up all 200 toothpicks and to spread them out over a designated area of grass (your front lawn, a section of a park or the outfield of the high school baseball field, for example). The area should be approximately 25 yards by 25 yards square.
2. Have your partner time you to see how many toothpicks you can pick up in 1 minute, in 2 minutes and in 3 minutes.

What happens:

After several trials, you probably noticed that you were able to locate and pick up more red toothpicks than green toothpicks. That's because the green toothpicks were more similar in color to the green color of the surrounding environment (the grass) than were the red ones. Thus, it was more difficult for you to locate the green toothpicks. Animals that are able to blend into their environment have a greater chance for survival than animals that do not blend in. The ability of animals to "match" the colors of their surroundings aids in their protection and survival. Green lizards are able to survive better in an area with lots of plants than are red or yellow lizards. Their predators (animals that would eat them) have a difficult time locating them.

Mimicry

Mimicry is the ability of one species to imitate the coloration or behavior of another species. This is a form of protection. Some animals, insects for example, are very distasteful or dangerous and thus are avoided by larger animals. Other types of insects have "adopted" the colors and body movements of those dangerous "models" and are able to escape detection by some of their enemies. For example, one type of fly looks exactly like a dangerous and poisonous wasp; one very tasty butterfly looks just like a not-so-tasty moth; and one caterpillar has body markings that make it look like the eyes of a giant bird. Mimicry allows some animals to survive simply because they look like other, more dangerous animals.

Life in the rainforest is tough. To survive, animals have developed a variety of adaptations that help them live and prosper. With millions of species competing for food and space, learning to survive may be the most important lesson any young animal receives.

2 The Forest Floor

Across the floor of the rainforest an impressive variety of living things crawl, work and grow. Be careful! Over there lies a *fer-de-lance snake,* one of the most poisonous snakes in the world. She's silently waiting for a small mouse to wander by. Then she will strike, sinking her fangs deep into the flesh of the hapless victim. Within a few minutes the creature will become a welcome meal for the *fer-de-lance,* who will eventually slither back into the layer of leaves.

The Forest Floor Checklist

▲ There is a lot of animal life on top of and beneath the forest floor.

▲ There is a wide variety of plants.

▲ There are billions and billions of microscopic organisms.

▲ The soil is very thin and poor in nutrients.

▲ The soil is unable to hold large quantities of water.

▲ Weather conditions are hot and humid.

▲ Very little sunlight reaches the forest floor.

Beetles, termites, ants and centipedes travel along the forest floor. If you look carefully, you will note that some of these insects have their own "highways" throughout the forest. Millions and millions of ants travel through the forest in columns that are miles long. A parade of ants will cross a stream or river by linking their legs together, one after the other, until they reach the other side.

Parade of Ants

23

Others will continue to link up until a living bridge is formed over the river. The rest of the ant colony then crawls over the bodies of their comrades to the other side.

Nearby, an army of leaf-cutter ants crawl out of their nest and begin climbing up a tree. Like miniature surgeons, they chew off parts of large leaves with their sharp mouths and parade back to their nest. Here, other members of the colony will chew the leaves into a mush. The mush is used to grow a fungus on which the colony will feed.

Ant Hotel

Have you ever wondered how ants build their tunnels in the soil? Here's an activity where you can watch that happen.

You'll need:

a large glass jar (A pickle jar works well.)
loose or sandy soil
large container of water (A large baking pan is fine.)
black construction paper
sugar water (Use 2 teaspoons of sugar mixed into a glass of water.)
small bits of fruit (e.g., apple)

1. Go outside and locate a rotting piece of wood (an old tree) or an area with lots of ants.
2. Scoop up some of the soil in the area and place it into the glass jar. Allow the ants to crawl onto a stick and shake them into the jar. (Try to get at least 50 ants.)
3. When you get home, place the jar in the middle of the baking pan that has been filled with 1 or 2 inches of water. This will prevent the ants from escaping into your house.
4. Sprinkle a couple of drops of sugar water on the soil and place some small bits of fruit on the surface.
5. Cover the glass jar on all sides, top and bottom, with the black construction paper so that it is completely dark inside the jar.
6. Every 6 or 7 days lift the paper to observe how the ants have built tunnels near the sides of the glass jar. Occasionally, sprinkle more sugar water over the surface and replenish the bits of fruit.
7. Return the ants to their original environment after a few weeks.

What happens:

The ants are able to build tunnels near the sides of the jar much as they do in the rainforest. You also notice that the ants are constantly busy and that they are all working together to keep the small "colony" running. Ant colonies in the rainforest, with millions of members, can create or destroy parts of their environment with alarming speed.

Ants are quite important in the ecology of the rainforest. By getting rid of dead or dying organisms they help keep the floor of the rainforest clean. Of course, some ants are known for their fierce behavior. Army ants, for example, will often attack animals much larger than they are—mice, lizards and caterpillars. Imagine having a million ants crawling over your body and you get an idea of how a mouse feels being attacked by a whole army of these creatures.

Learning Log

You may be surprised to discover the wide variety of life that lives near your house. Besides ants, you may discover an exciting array of flora and fauna that you normally wouldn't notice.

Find an old log in a field, woods or park near where you live. Carefully examine it from one end to the other. Make a study of its decay as well as of the different plants and animals that cover its surface. Take notes or photographs over a period of time (several months, if possible) of the different organisms (for example, fungi, bacteria, insects, ants, mushrooms, lichens and so on) that cover its surface. How much or how little do you discover? Are there certain types of organisms that predominate? Are there certain times of the day or the year in which certain organisms appear or disappear? What can you predict will happen to the log in five years? Twenty-five years?

Look carefully and you'll see an abundant variety of organic matter littering the floor of the rainforest. Leaves, branches, fallen trees, flowers, fruit and other types of plant life cover the ground. These dead and decaying materials are quickly converted into nutrients for the rapidly growing plants nearby. This litter is efficiently recycled by billions of microscopic decomposers living in the soil. This process is so efficient that the lower layer of soil has little mineral content. In fact, most of the forest's mineral wealth is stored in the vegetation growing throughout the rainforest.

Banana Bags

Decomposition, or the natural decay of dead organisms, is a natural process in nature. Here's how you can watch it happen in your own home.

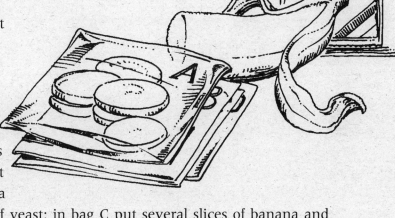

You'll need:

four plastic sandwich bags
a banana
dry packaged yeast
water

Label each of the four sealable plastic sandwich bags A, B, C and D. In bag A put several slices of banana; in bag B put several slices of banana and empty in a packet of yeast; in bag C put several slices of banana and some water; and in bag D put several slices of banana, some water and a packet of yeast. Seal all the bags and place them on a sunny windowsill.

What happens:

After 3 or 4 days you will notice the following:

1. The banana slices in bag A will darken slightly.
2. The yeast in bag B will grow very slowly, but there will be little change.

3. The banana slices in bag C will show some decay and some mold.
4. The banana slices in bag D will show the most decay. The banana will be breaking down; the liquid will be bubbling; carbon dioxide gas will be forming inside the bag and the bag may even pop open releasing a powerful odor into the room.

When plants and animals die, their bodies serve as a valuable food source for many microorganisms. These microorganisms feed on the bodies, breaking them down. Yeast is composed of millions of microorganisms that are able to grow when the right conditions (moisture, food and warmth) are present. As they grow, they break down the banana slices. The same process takes place in nature. As a result, the microorganisms can reduce large animals and plants into valuable nutrients for the soil. In other words, when an organism dies it provides life for other organisms.

As you might expect, the soil in the rainforest is quite different from the soil you might find in your backyard. The materials in soil, the depth of soil and its color vary considerably from one area to the next. Rainforest soil is filled with an abundance of organic life, yet it is very thin. The soil in your part of the world may be thick and rich with humus or thin and dry with sand.

Soil Shake

Have you ever wondered what soil really is? What's all the stuff in soil? Why are some soils good and other soils poor? Here's a project that will help you learn the answers to those questions.

You'll need:

several large glass jars (Mayonnaise jars work well.)
a hand trowel
    soil from different areas around your community

1. Take several jars and visit separate sites in and around your local community (your backyard, a park, behind a gas station, the corner of a garden, for example).
2. Using the hand trowel dig for a sample of soil and place it in a jar, one sample of soil per jar.
3. When you get home fill each of the jars three-quarters full with water and shake each jar vigorously for about 30 seconds.
4. Allow the jars to sit undisturbed for several days.

What happens:

Soil is composed of many things (dead plants and animals, minerals, water, air, humus [the decomposition of organic matter] and millions of microscopic organisms). The composition of soil (or the ratio of humus and minerals) will determine its ability to grow various types of plants. Some soil is poor in nutrients and will not be able to support a rich variety of plant life. On the other hand,

29

soil that is composed of lots of organic matter can and does support lots of plants. The soil for our gardens and the soil necessary for growing certain crops usually has lots of organic matter.

As you see in this project, there are many different types of soil. Typically, soil will be composed of four or five separate layers, as in the illustration at right.

In the rainforest, the soil is so poor that the top layer (the layer in which most of the plants grow) is thin. Thus, not many nutrients are available for plants to use. In this project, you may have discovered soil that had a thick layer of humus (garden soil, for example) and soil that had a thin layer of humus. Which of your samples would be most similar to rainforest soil?

— WATER

— HUMUS
— CLAY
— SILT
— SAND
— COARSE SAND AND GRAVEL

The soil of the rainforest decomposes very rapidly. This is one of the main reasons why the soil is so thin. High temperatures, high humidity and many microorganisms in the soil contribute to this decomposition process.

If you could bring a microscope into the rainforest and look at a sample of soil under the lens, you would see an incredible variety of tiny organisms living beneath the surface. These include microscopic bacteria as well as an abundance of other creatures that feed on the organic matter that constantly falls to the forest floor. These organisms are known as *decomposers*. You would also see an amazing assortment of subterranean fungi throughout your soil sample. These fungi (in the same family as mushrooms) are important to the growth of rainforest plants because they help the plants absorb minerals in the soil. The decomposers convert the plant litter into minerals, and the fungi assist plants by transferring those minerals into their roots. The damp, humid conditions of the rainforest also contribute to the rapid growth and reproduction of these organisms. All this organic matter combines to form a mix that is constantly being broken down, converted and used. It is a never-ending cycle.

Root Routes

If the soil of the rainforest is so thin, how are plants able to get the nutrients and water they need to grow? Here's an activity that will show you the answer.

You'll need:

2 2-liter clear plastic soda bottles
potting soil
coarse sand (You can buy this at a local hardware store.)
bean and radish seeds

1. Poke several tiny holes in the bottom of each plastic bottle. Cut the top off each one, too. Fill each of the 2 bottles half full with an equal amount of sand. Label the bottles 1 and 2.
2. In the first bottle put a layer of potting soil 3 inches deep. In the second bottle put a layer of potting soil 1 inch deep.
3. In each bottle plant some bean and radish seeds along the plastic sides so you can observe the roots growing. Place the seeds approximately three-quarters of an inch below the surface of the potting soil.
4. Place the bottles in a sunny location and water frequently. After several days the seeds will germinate and begin to grow.

What happens:

After several days you will be able to see how the root systems of the bean and radish plants are developing. The roots of the plants in bottle 1 are able to penetrate deeper into the soil to obtain the necessary nutrients and water. The roots of the plants in bottle 2 need to spread out to obtain their nutrients. Because of the thin layer of soil in bottle 2, the root structures of the plants have "adapted" to their environment in order to survive.

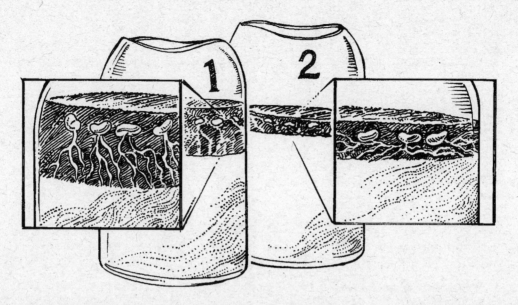

The thin layer of soil in the rainforest means that the roots of the plants that live there must spread out to take in the necessary nutrients and water.

Also crawling in and through the soil is a wide variety of larger creatures. These include thousands of earthworms, creatures able to convert organic litter into soil. Earthworms do this by eating the dead leaves, passing the material through their bodies and turning it into humus. This humus provides some of the nutrients for plant growth. By crawling through the soil, earthworms also aerate the soil. In order for water to pass through the soil and reach the roots of plants, there must be sufficient spaces between the particles of soil. Earthworms and other soil creatures accomplish this as they travel through the soil—eating their way through all the litter.

Worm World

Worms are an important part of the decomposition process. Not only do they eat organic matter in the soil, they also aerate the soil. Here's an activity that will allow you to see how that happens.

You'll need:

several large glass jars
soil
gravel
dead leaves
earthworms (These can be dug from someone's yard or purchased from a local bait shop.)

1. Wash and rinse several large glass jars.
2. In the bottom of each place a layer of clean gravel and several inches of loose soil. Sprinkle some dead leaves over the soil and moisten with a little water.
3. Place several earthworms in each jar. Wrap a piece of black paper around each jar. (Worms prefer to work in darkness and will tend to build their tunnels near the glass sides when light is kept out of their "home.")
4. Every few days or so remove the black paper to observe the tunnels made by the worms, as well as their movements. The soil should be sprinkled occasionally, also. After a few weeks, the worms should be let loose in a garden area.

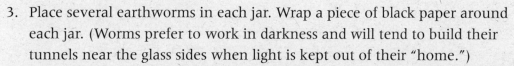

What happens:

The earthworms will eat their way through the organic matter in the jar. As they do, they aerate the soil and convert the organic matter into humus. In this way the nutrients in that matter can be used by plants.

Across the forest floor, you would also see the young and tender shoots of many plants poking out of the soil. These plants are usually small and delicate. Seedlings, ferns and mushrooms can be found along with sprouts, mosses and lichens. Because very little sunlight is able to reach the floor of the forest, the small plants that grow there require little light. Indeed, only about 2 percent of the sunlight that shines on the canopy reaches the forest floor. Unfortunately, competition for the nutrients in the soil is fierce. As a result, little of this young vegetation will develop into tall trees or other mature plants. For every tree that reaches maturity, hundreds of seedlings fail to survive.

Hold On!

The soil of the rainforest rarely washes away—even after a heavy rainstorm. This is because there are so many plants, and the roots of these plants hold the soil in place. Here's an activity that will show you how this works.

You'll need:

bean seeds
potting soil
a small flower pot (with a drainage hole)

1. Fill the flower pot with potting soil (almost to the top). Follow the seed packet directions and plant about 5 to 7 seeds in the pot.
2. Water the soil in the pot and place it in a sunny location. Follow the seed packet directions and water the seeds regularly.

3. After several days, the seeds will begin to spout and grow. Continue to water and provide necessary sunlight.

4. After about 5 to 6 weeks the bean plants will be well on their way. Hold onto the pot with one hand and grasp all the bean plants gently with the other hand. Gently separate the flower pot from the plants.

What happens:

When the flower pot is removed, most of the soil remains in the shape of the flower pot. This is because the roots of the bean plants have woven their way throughout the soil, holding it all together. In this way, the roots trap the particles of soil so that they cannot be washed away by water. The plants can then take in the nutrients in the soil and continue their growth process. Because there are so many plants (and so many roots throughout the soil) the soil cannot be washed away during the many rainstorms occurring in rainforest areas. (Note: Be sure to separate your bean plants and transplant them to a garden outside so that you can enjoy the beans when they fully mature.)

If you were careful, you would be able to see a wide variety of amazing creatures on the forest floor. These would include rabbits, tapirs, pacas, agoutis, deer and frogs. As you will discover in a later chapter, the frogs of the rainforest are some of the most amazing creatures ever. While many frogs live up in the trees, there are several varieties of frogs that live in the small pools and decaying plant matter of the forest floor. There is plenty of activity taking place on the floor of the rainforest. Rich in both plant and animal life, the soil teems with an abundance of organisms on its surface as well as underground. Perhaps nowhere else on the planet is there such an amazing and incredible diversity of life.

As you can see, the floor of the rainforest is alive with many creatures, many plants and a complex assembly of processes and procedures. It is an ideal environment that not only teems with life, but provides an abundance of life for its inhabitants. As you'll discover in succeeding chapters of this book, the forest floor in combination with the other layers of the rainforest is an ecologically diverse world, quite different, yet also similar, to the environment in which you live.

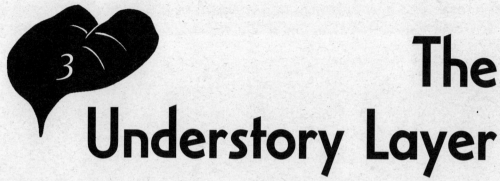

The Understory Layer

The chatter of brightly colored birds echoes throughout the rainforest. Curled in a low hanging branch, an ocelot sleeps—unconcerned about the noise around him. Broad leaves hang down and trap the few slices of sunlight that reach this portion of the rainforest. Life in many forms abounds in this section of the rainforest—sometimes noisy, sometimes quiet—but always full of surprises.

The Understory Checklist

▲ Little sunlight reaches this part of the rainforest.
▲ It is damp and humid.
▲ Trees seldom grow to more that 30 feet in height.
▲ There is plenty of vegetation and wildlife.
▲ Mosses and algae thrive.
▲ Plants often have large, broad leaves.
▲ There is a wide variety of insect life.

Understory Plants

The understory is filled with plants that grow very little each year. Most of the plants in this part of the rainforest reach heights of 5 to 30 feet. Since very little sunlight reaches this part of the rainforest, the plants do not have sufficient light to grow big and tall. As a result, some of the trees are immature specimens of the larger and taller trees in the canopy. Whenever a large tree (from the canopy or emergent layer) dies and falls over, however, it pulls down or topples several other nearby plants. When that happens, sunlight is able to penetrate the opening left by the fallen tree. The sunlight warms this section of the rainforest. That's when many understory plants begin to grow very rapidly.

Sunlight is very important in the life cycle of the rainforest. Many plants can't do without it, while others are able to survive and grow with just a minimum of light or no light at all. This is part of the biological process, known as *adaptation,* in which features or behaviors that help an organism survive in a particular place evolve over a period of years, decades or centuries.

Plants in the understory layer are able to grow in that type of environment because they have "learned" how to live with a minimum amount of sunlight. By the same token, these plants are able to take advantage of the small bits of sunlight that infrequently penetrate to this damp and dark section of the rainforest.

Light Travel

Plants will always grow toward a light source. Here's an experiment that shows how this happens.

You'll need:

2 shoe boxes
a healthy plant (such as a bean plant)

1. Cut 2 pieces of cardboard from one of the shoe boxes.
2. Tape the pieces inside the other shoe box as in the following illustration.
3. Cut a hole in the top of the box. Place a healthy plant (a growing bean plant works well) in the bottom of the box and place the lid over the box.
4. Place the shoe box in a sunny location. Every other day or so remove the lid and water the plant.

What happens:

The plant will grow toward the light source, bending around the cardboard pieces to do so.

Since many green plants can grow faster when sunlight is available, they will "take advantage" of any sunlight possible. Plants in the rainforest, just like plants everywhere, use a process known as *phototropism*—a natural process in which plants will grow in the direction of any light source. In your experiment, the plant grew toward the sunlight, even bending around the cardboard pieces to do so. The same thing happens in the rainforest when a large tree falls and allows some sunlight to reach the depths of the rainforest.

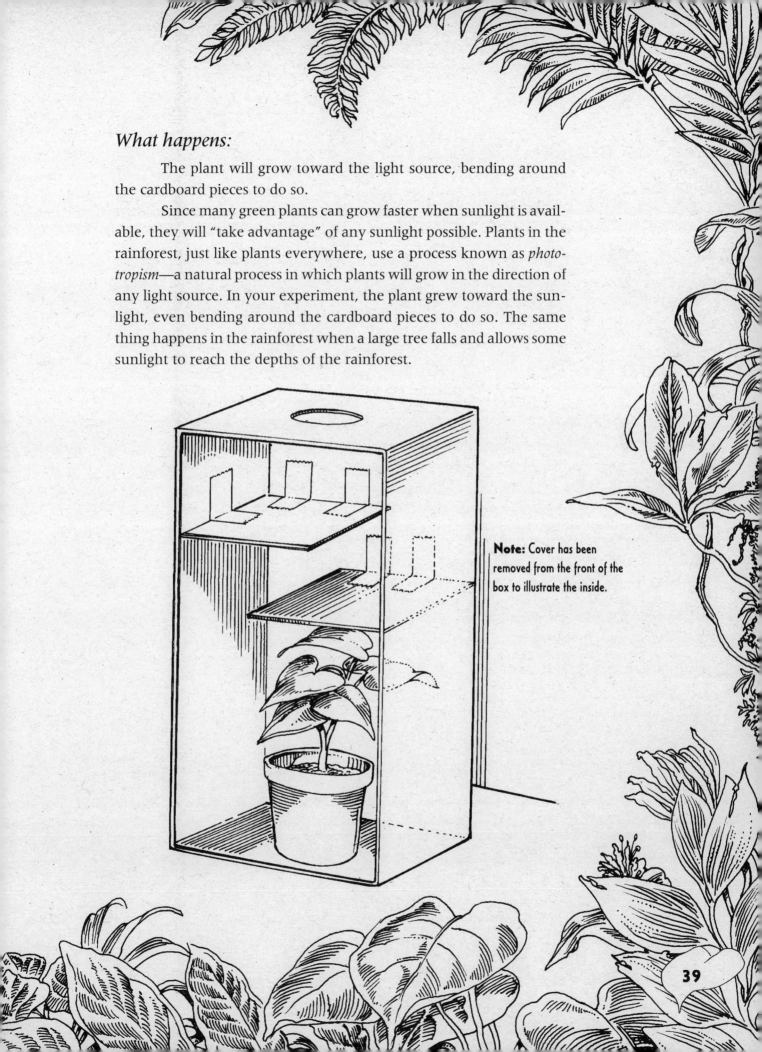

Note: Cover has been removed from the front of the box to illustrate the inside.

Bromeliads

Bromeliads are plants that grow in both the understory and canopy layers of the rainforest. They are able to live on the branches and trunks of many rainforest trees. Most amazing is the fact that they do not need roots reaching into the soil to obtain the water and nutrients necessary for their survival.

These plants have developed a unique way of obtaining needed water and nutrients. Most of them have long curved leaves that overlap at the base—forming a tight little bowl at the bottom. The leaves act like gutters to collect the falling rain and the "tank" holds the water. Some bromeliads are able to hold up to 2 gallons of water.

The pools of water are also home to many varieties of animals such as frogs, insects, worms and spiders. Scientists have discovered more than 250 different species of animals in the "tanks" of bromeliads. The animals leave their droppings in the tanks, providing nourishment to the plants. When these animals die, their bodies contribute to the plants' growth as well.

Tropical Treat

Here is an activity that will help you learn about the role of bromeliads in the rainforest.

You'll need:

    a fresh pineapple
    a sharp knife (to be used by an adult only)
    soil
    a large pot

1. Go to a large grocery store and select a pineapple with healthy green leaves.
2. When you return home, have an adult cut off the top of the pineapple, leaving about 3 inches of fruit attached to the leaves.
3. Allow the pineapple top to dry for a day or two. Remove the soft fruit, but leave the core attached to the leaves.
4. Fill the pot with soil and plant the pineapple top with the core in the soil and the leaves above the soil. Be sure to water the pineapple plant.
5. Set the plant in a sunny location outdoors. Make sure the temperature outside is warm enough. Water it whenever the soil becomes dry.

What happens:

After a rainstorm, check the pineapple plant and notice what is collecting in the center of the plant or at the base of its leaves. Look for small pools of water, particles of dirt, or animal life.

Keep observing the pineapple plant over a period of several weeks. What new discoveries can you make in the leaves of the plant? Although rainforest bromeliads have larger "pools" than you will find in a pineapple, you should be able to notice a rich variety of life collecting in your plant. Imagine what you might find in a 2-gallon "pool"!

The twilight world of the understory is ideal for many plants and animals. It's not unusual for this part of the rainforest to have high levels of humidity. In fact, the amount of moisture in the air rarely falls below 95 percent.

Climatic conditions contribute to the high humidity, but the abundance of plants also has an effect on the amount of water in the air, too. All green plants make their food through a process known as *photosynthesis*. In this process light from the sun combines with water and carbon dioxide (what you exhale when you breathe) to create sugar for a plant's growth. A byproduct of this process is the release of oxygen (which you need to live) and water. The release of water into the air is known as *transpiration*. As you might imagine, when there are a lot of plants in a particular area, there will be a lot of oxygen and water released into the air. By the same token, when large numbers of plants are removed from an area there is a decrease in the amount of oxygen and water released into the surrounding environment.

One of the reasons why so many scientists are concerned about the destruction of the world's rainforests is the effect that destruction will have on the world's oxygen supply. Many scientists believe that more than 50 percent of the world's oxygen supply is generated by the plants of the rainforest. When those plants are eliminated, so is an important source of oxygen.

The following activity will provide you with an opportunity to see part of this process in action—specifically, how plants release water vapor into the air. Keep in mind that there are millions of plants in the rainforest transpiring water, whereas in your part of the country there may only be a few hundred or thousand plants.

Into the Air

Water several potted plants thoroughly. Place a dry plastic bag loosely over one or more of the branches and leaves of each plant for several hours. Record the time. Observe the plant every hour and record what happens inside the bag.

Place plastic bags around several live branches of different trees outside and secure each one with a piece of string. If possible, put bags on some branches that are in direct sunlight and other bags on branches that are in shade. Leave the bags on for several hours. Carefully remove the bags and measure the amount of water in each one. Compare your results from different trees and from different sites on an individual tree. You may also want to do this activity at various times during the day. (Do plants transpire more water in the morning or in the evening?) Conduct this activity throughout the year and observe your results. (Do plants transpire more water in the summer or in the winter?)

Food Feast

A wide variety of foods and food products can be found in the rainforest. Many of these products are harvested from plants and trees that compose the understory layer of the forest. In fact, you may have several of these foods in your home right now. Check to see how many of the following items are in your kitchen.

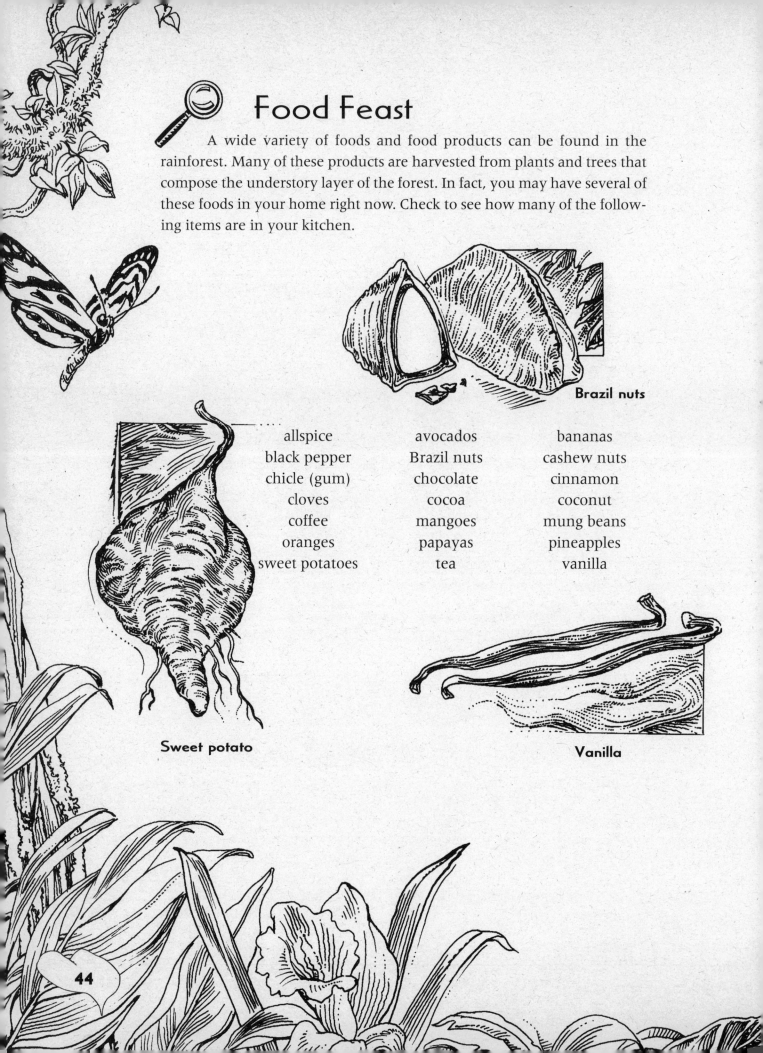

Brazil nuts

allspice	avocados	bananas
black pepper	Brazil nuts	cashew nuts
chicle (gum)	chocolate	cinnamon
cloves	cocoa	coconut
coffee	mangoes	mung beans
oranges	papayas	pineapples
sweet potatoes	tea	vanilla

Sweet potato

Vanilla

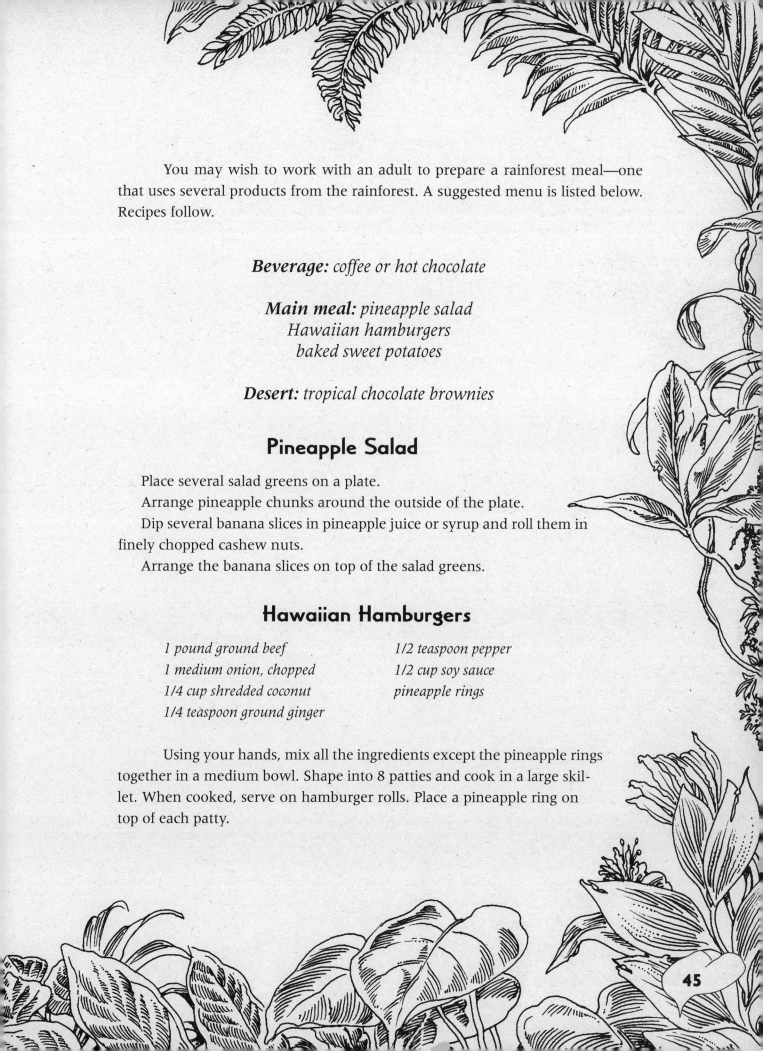

You may wish to work with an adult to prepare a rainforest meal—one that uses several products from the rainforest. A suggested menu is listed below. Recipes follow.

Beverage: *coffee or hot chocolate*

Main meal: *pineapple salad*
Hawaiian hamburgers
baked sweet potatoes

Desert: *tropical chocolate brownies*

Pineapple Salad

Place several salad greens on a plate.
Arrange pineapple chunks around the outside of the plate.
Dip several banana slices in pineapple juice or syrup and roll them in finely chopped cashew nuts.
Arrange the banana slices on top of the salad greens.

Hawaiian Hamburgers

1 pound ground beef   *1/2 teaspoon pepper*
1 medium onion, chopped   *1/2 cup soy sauce*
1/4 cup shredded coconut   *pineapple rings*
1/4 teaspoon ground ginger

Using your hands, mix all the ingredients except the pineapple rings together in a medium bowl. Shape into 8 patties and cook in a large skillet. When cooked, serve on hamburger rolls. Place a pineapple ring on top of each patty.

Baked Sweet Potatoes

sweet potatoes
aluminum foil

Place sweet potatoes wrapped in aluminum foil in oven and bake at 350° for 45 minutes.

Tropical Chocolate Brownies

2 squares unsweetened chocolate   *1 cup sifted flour*
1 cup sugar   *1 teaspoon baking powder*
2 tablespoons butter   *1/2 cup evaporated milk*
1 egg   *1 cup chopped Brazil nuts*
1 teaspoon vanilla

Preheat oven to 350°F. Place the chocolate in a small pan and heat slowly over low heat. (Be careful not to burn it.) Put the sugar, butter, egg and vanilla into a medium bowl and mix until well blended. Pour the melted chocolate into the sugar-butter mixture and blend thoroughly. Sift the flour and baking powder together in a separate bowl and stir half of the mixture in with the sugar-butter mixture. Add the evaporated milk and stir the batter until smooth. Sift in the rest of the flour and add the chopped nuts—stirring until all lumps have disappeared.

Pour the batter into a 9-inch square, greased pan. Bake for 30 minutes. Remove and allow to cool. When cooled, cut into squares and enjoy.

Understory Animals

The understory is filled with a wide variety of small and large animals. As you might imagine, the competition for food and space is intense. Just surviving from one day to the next can be an overwhelming task.

Rainforest animals have developed a number of "strategies" that help them survive. You may wish to re-read the part on "adaptation" mentioned earlier in chapter 1. One of the most common is known as *camouflage*, the ability of an animal to use its shape or colors to look like something else in the environment. Frequently, animals will hide to avoid being eaten by other animals. Other animals can disguise themselves so they can sneak up on their food and capture it. Finding food to eat and not becoming food for another animal is how animals survive the harsh world of the rainforest.

Let's take a look at some of the rainforest animals that live and hide in the understory.

Walking Stick

Have you ever seen a stick walking through the forest? There are about 2,000 species of stick insects throughout the world, most of them living in the rainforest. When walking, these curious creatures look like animated twigs. When still, they look like an extension of a branch or stick. In fact, they can remain motionless for several hours, completely fooling predators looking for a tasty meal.

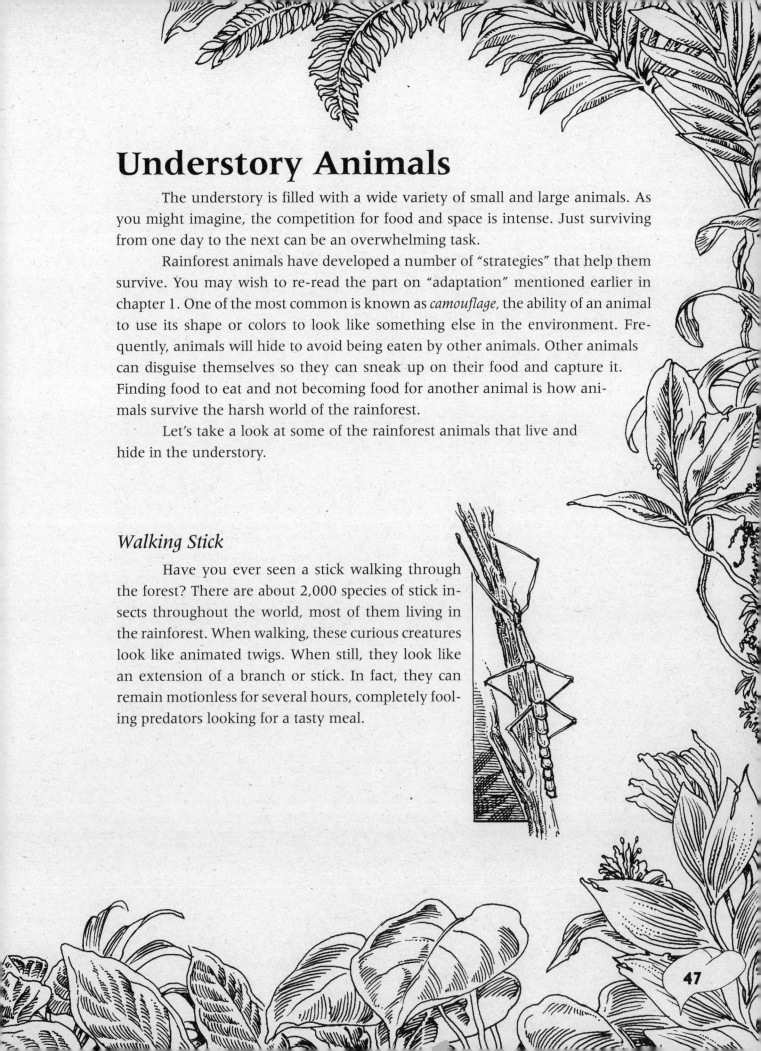

Leaf Frog

A frog that looks like a leaf! This curiously shaped amphibian lives in the rainforests of Southeast Asia. Its brownish color and extra folds of skin help it look like a large leaf lying on the ground. There, it is able to hide among dead leaves and other plant life waiting for small insects and other jungle creatures to pass by. It quickly snaps up any animal that gets too close.

Windowpane Butterfly

Wouldn't it be amazing to see completely through the body of your family cat or dog? The wings of the windowpane butterfly, which lives in South American rainforests, are completely transparent. Two violet-colored spots on the wings make this animal look like the flowers on which it rests. Larger insects, which like to eat butterflies, pass this animal by, thinking it's just another pretty jungle blossom.

Grasshopper

If you were walking in the rainforests of Southeast Asia, you would have to be very careful where you stepped because of all the animals that live on the forest floor. One of the most cleverly disguised creatures is the grasshopper, an insect that looks just like a fallen leaf. Because of its size and shape this animal can hide from all its enemies, none of which bother with something that looks like a dead leaf.

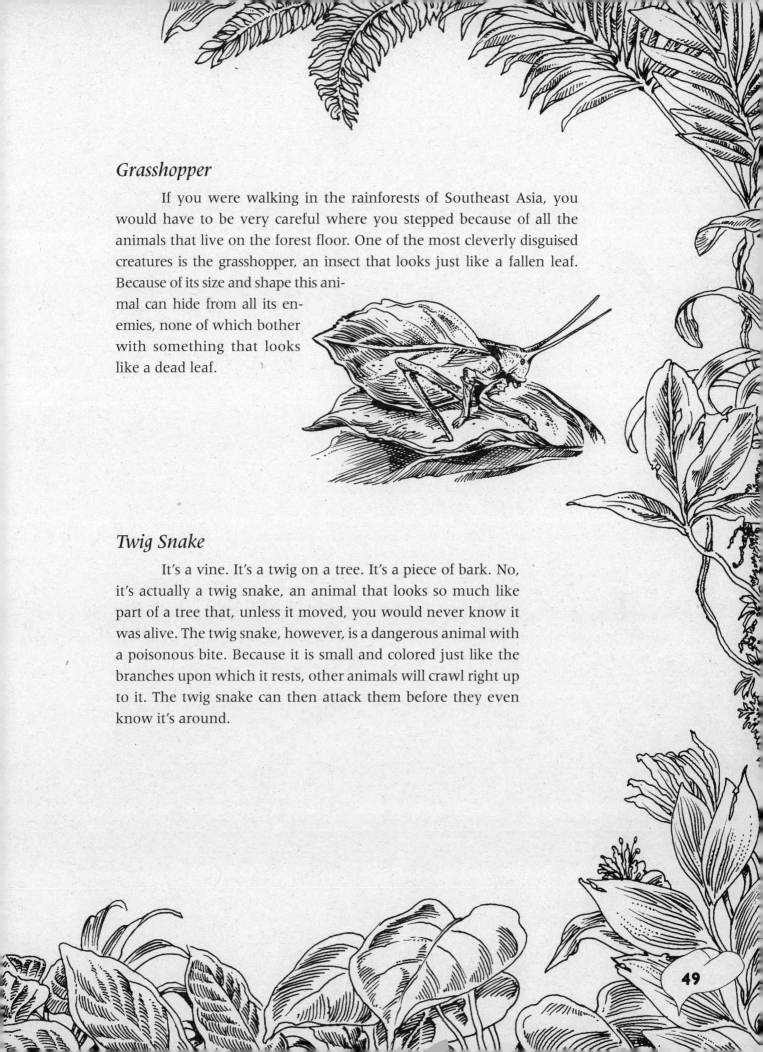

Twig Snake

It's a vine. It's a twig on a tree. It's a piece of bark. No, it's actually a twig snake, an animal that looks so much like part of a tree that, unless it moved, you would never know it was alive. The twig snake, however, is a dangerous animal with a poisonous bite. Because it is small and colored just like the branches upon which it rests, other animals will crawl right up to it. The twig snake can then attack them before they even know it's around.

Gecko

If you put a gecko in the middle of your living room, it would look like a creature from another world. But the barklike markings on the skin of this creature make it look exactly like tree bark. Its brown and gray skin allows it to hide on branches and tree trunks so that it is practically invisible. When tasty insects fly too close, the gecko can easily capture them for a satisfying meal.

Leaf Insect

You would probably have a difficult time locating any of these insects in the rainforests of Australia or Southeast Asia. That's because these extraordinary creatures look like real leaves.

These incredible animals, which are related to stick insects, camouflage themselves by their shape and color. Their bodies have markings and wing veins that resemble the veins of a living leaf. Young leaf insects are usually green, imitating the small green leaves on which they feed. Adult leaf insects are often brown or speckled, which help them look like the dying leaves of forest trees. There are some leaf insects that can change their colors daily, becoming light colored in the day and dark colored at night.

New Guinea Beetles

This creature can grow its own camouflage! These beetles, which are found in the damp rainforests of New Guinea, have a variety of plant life growing all over their bodies. Their skin is pitted with holes and crevices that hold tiny amounts of water. Lichens, fungi and mosses are able to grow in these holes and completely cover the beetles. Look down and you may see tiny "gardens" crawling across the floor of a New Guinea forest.

Frogmouth Bird

What an unusual name for a bird! This creature, which lives in Australia, rests on the trunks of giant rainforest trees. As long as it doesn't move, it looks exactly like a tree trunk. If it is disturbed, however, it protects itself by quickly opening its large mouth and scaring away any nearby intruders.

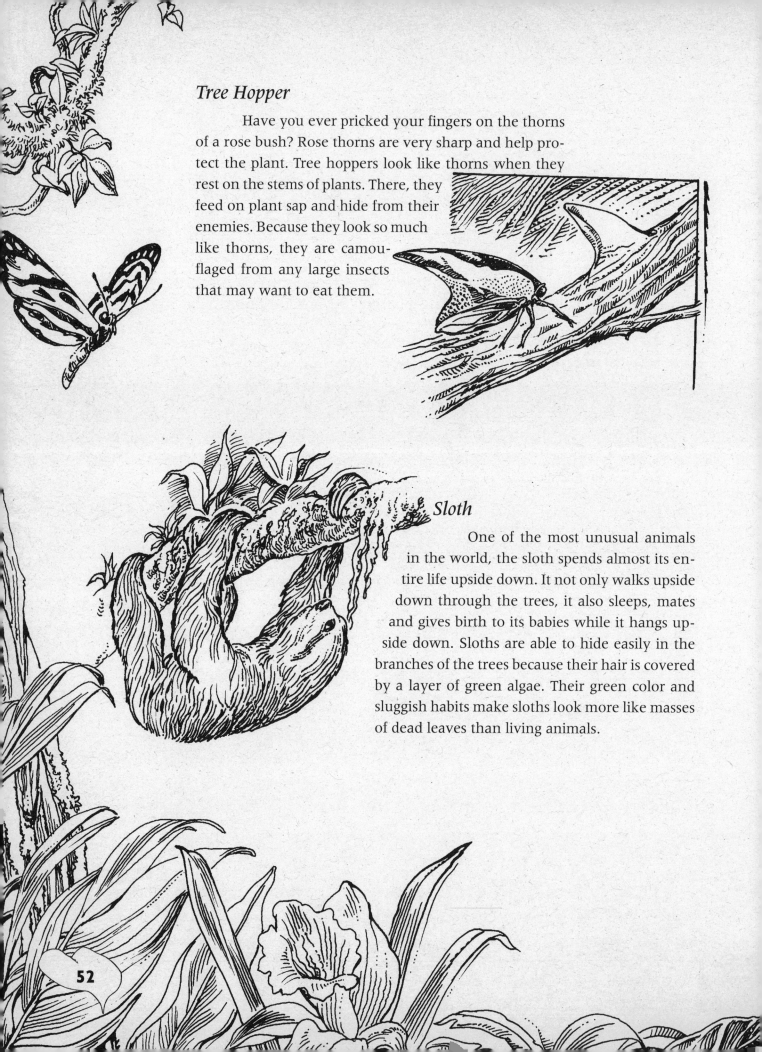

Tree Hopper

Have you ever pricked your fingers on the thorns of a rose bush? Rose thorns are very sharp and help protect the plant. Tree hoppers look like thorns when they rest on the stems of plants. There, they feed on plant sap and hide from their enemies. Because they look so much like thorns, they are camouflaged from any large insects that may want to eat them.

Sloth

One of the most unusual animals in the world, the sloth spends almost its entire life upside down. It not only walks upside down through the trees, it also sleeps, mates and gives birth to its babies while it hangs upside down. Sloths are able to hide easily in the branches of the trees because their hair is covered by a layer of green algae. Their green color and sluggish habits make sloths look more like masses of dead leaves than living animals.

52

Peacock Butterfly

To protect itself from its enemies, the peacock butterfly has dull brown wings. These help it blend in with the bark of several trees. But this insect has another survival trick. When it opens its wings, there are four large markings that look like giant eyes. These "eyes" scare away any animal trying to turn the peacock butterfly into a tasty meal.

Great Potoo

A bird that looks like a tree! The great potoo is a remarkable animal that lives in the rainforests of South America. It is able to land on the trunk of a tree, sit very still for long periods of time and look just like another plant. Its brown feathers are colored exactly like tree bark, and its ability to remain motionless helps it stay virtually undetected among all the other plants.

The animals you met are camouflaged for good reasons. They need to find food or avoid becoming food for other creatures. These animals are able to hide because their colors or shapes help them look like something else.

Scientists tell us that the colors and shapes of some animals have come about (or evolved) over thousands or millions of years. An animal is able to survive because it has adapted to its environment; it knows how to find its food and what to do to hide from its enemies. Camouflage helps animals live and survive in the harsh world of the rainforest.

The Canopy Layer

Quick … look over there! It's a group of toucans flashing through the trees. Glance beyond them and you'll see a small band of squirrel monkeys darting over and under branches. Listen … do you hear that? It's the slithering of an anaconda snake over the bark of a kapok tree. Watch carefully and you'll observe a rainbow of bright colors as a swarm of morpho butterflies floats up and over the treetops.

This is the third layer of the rainforest—the canopy layer. This layer is more active and more alive than any other layer. Indeed, more animals live and make their homes in this part of the rainforest than in any other section. It's filled with an assortment of sounds, colors, shapes and sizes that you would never find in any zoo or even in a collection of zoos. Welcome to the canopy layer!

The Canopy Layer Checklist

- ▲ The canopy is formed by a thick layer of vegetation.
- ▲ Ninety-eight percent of the sunlight that strikes the rainforest is blocked out by the canopy.
- ▲ Trees in this layer reach heights of 65 to 100 feet.
- ▲ "Hanging gardens" overflow with an enormous variety of plant life.
- ▲ Most rainforest animals make their homes in the canopy layer.

Filled with sights, sounds and colors, the canopy layer is truly amazing! Screeching, clawing, howling and whirring are common sounds to this part of the rainforest. Swinging monkeys, swooping birds, climbing frogs and lazy sloths make their way through the thick vegetation. Reds, yellows, greens, blues and a host of other bright colors flash throughout the treetops like an endless parade of Christmas lights.

An Important Canopy Animal

While you have met several rainforest animals in this book, let's take a more detailed look at one we have already met. This animal not only inhabits the canopy and understory layers of the rainforest, but it is also synonymous with some of the problems associated with many rainforests around the world.

The Sloth

The sloth is an animal living in the rainforest canopy. It spends most of its life hanging upside down in trees. It even sleeps upside down! Sloths are so adapted to life in the trees that they cannot survive on the ground. Sloths are also known as one of the slowest moving animals in the world. The fur of the sloth is covered with algae or other microscopic plants, giving it a green color. Thus, it is very easily camouflaged in the branches of trees.

The three-toed sloth is hunted by natives for its meat. Because it moves so slowly it is killed easily. The sloth is also threatened by the destruction of the Amazon rainforest. The sloth only eats the cecropia plant, and when that plant is destroyed, the sloth cannot find anything else to eat.

Did You Know?

- The three-toed sloth can travel no faster than 4 feet per minute.
- The sloth sleeps for about 20 hours each day.
- The fur on a sloth grows from its belly to its spine, the opposite direction of most land animals.
- The sloth has black, enamelless teeth.
- The two-toed sloth is more common than the three-toed sloth and is the type usually found in zoos.
- Because it spends its entire life in the trees, a sloth is virtually unable to move on the ground.
- As the Brazilian rainforest is destroyed, so is the habitat of the sloth.

The sloth is important because it represents one of the most serious problems facing the rainforests in general and the animals of the canopy in particular. The sloth, like many other rainforest animals, is an *endangered species*. An endangered species is one that is in danger of dying out completely, never to return again. We refer to this process as extinction. When an animal is extinct, it has ceased to survive and no one will ever see one again.

Extinction in nature is a natural process. In fact, many scientists have estimated that 99 percent of all the plant and animal species that have ever lived on the earth are now extinct. What is unfortunate is that humans are speeding up the extinction of several types of animals, placing many animals on endangered species lists. When these animals are gone they are gone forever.

As the population of the world increases so does the danger to the world's animals. Humans are moving into rainforest areas once dominated by animals. They are clearing the land for agricultural purposes and building houses for people to live in. They are constructing factories that pour chemicals into the air and nearby rivers. And they are hunting animals for sport or for pleasure. Whatever the reason, many animals are in danger of being eliminated from the face of the earth.

Did You Know?

- It has been estimated that one plant or animal species becomes extinct every 30 minutes.
- About 18 percent of all the bird species in the world are currently endangered.
- There are more bird species in the canopy layer of the rainforest than anywhere else on earth.

Field Trip

What are some of the different types of dwellings or "houses" in which animals live in your part of the world? Let's take a look.

You'll need:

a notebook
a camera and film

1. With a friend or an adult, take a walking "field trip" around your town or neighborhood. How many different animal homes can you locate? These may include nests, burrows, tree trunks, ant hills, rocks, logs, underground openings or even cracks in the sidewalk.
2. If possible, take a photograph or draw an illustration of each habitat.
3. When the photos are developed, try and match each picture with the name or an illustration of the animal that lives there.
4. You may want to have a high school or college student help you in matching animal homes with the occupants. How many different homes can you find in your neighborhood?

Animals live in a wide variety of homes, just like humans. Their homes may be high up in the trees or far beneath the ground. The homes that animals live in are designed to protect their young, offer them shelter from the weather, help them defend against their enemies or aid them in obtaining the food they need. In fact, aren't those the same reasons why humans live in houses?

BIRD

ANTS

Write Away!

You may be interested in constructing or obtaining one or more different animal habitats, some of which you can place outside your home for daily observation. Bird feeders and birdhouses, bug houses, aquariums, terrariums and the like would all be appropriate. Many larger toy stores sell a variety of animal habitats. You can also order animal homes from these mail-order houses:

Aquarium and Science Supply Company
101 Old York Road
Jenkintown, PA 19046
(800) 453-3333

Delta Education
P.O. Box 3000
Hudson, NH 03061
(800) 282-9560

Nasco
901 Janesville Avenue
Fort Atkinson, WI 53538
(800) 558-9595

Canopy Plants and Their Importance

Some of the most amazing plants in the rainforest can be found throughout the canopy layer. Just as there is such a wide variety of animal life in this region of the forest, so, too, is there an incredible array of plant life. Let's take a look at some of the remarkable vegetation of the canopy.

Epiphytes

An epiphyte is a tropical rainforest plant that grows on the branches or trunks of other plants. What is most unusual about these plants is that typically they have no roots whatsoever; they are able to take their food and water from the surrounding atmosphere. In short, these plants do not need soil to grow and thrive; they are able to get everything they need high up in the branches of the rainforest.

Epiphytes are also known as air plants since they grow so high up in the trees. Some epiphytes have air roots that absorb water right from the air; some are able to store water in their stems or in a small "cup" in the middle of the plant. They obtain their nutrients from the litter that falls down from the trees and the dust dissolved in rain water. They do not, however, cause any damage to the trees or other plants on which they grow. Examples of epiphytes include mosses and ferns. Orchids are also epiphytes, and there are more than 20,000 different types of orchids that grow in the tropical rainforests of the world.

To the Light

All plants grow toward a light source, particularly those in the rainforest. Here's an experiment that demonstrates how powerful that process is.

You'll need:

a small potted plant with a strong root system
2 large sponges
string

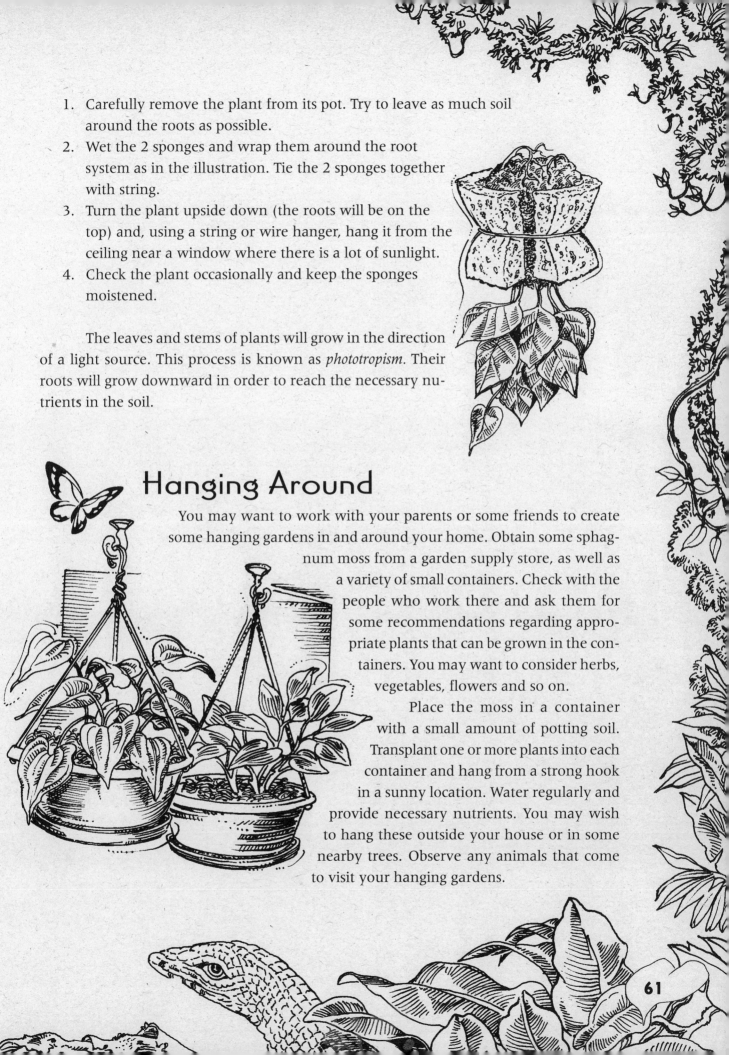

1. Carefully remove the plant from its pot. Try to leave as much soil around the roots as possible.
2. Wet the 2 sponges and wrap them around the root system as in the illustration. Tie the 2 sponges together with string.
3. Turn the plant upside down (the roots will be on the top) and, using a string or wire hanger, hang it from the ceiling near a window where there is a lot of sunlight.
4. Check the plant occasionally and keep the sponges moistened.

The leaves and stems of plants will grow in the direction of a light source. This process is known as *phototropism*. Their roots will grow downward in order to reach the necessary nutrients in the soil.

Hanging Around

You may want to work with your parents or some friends to create some hanging gardens in and around your home. Obtain some sphagnum moss from a garden supply store, as well as a variety of small containers. Check with the people who work there and ask them for some recommendations regarding appropriate plants that can be grown in the containers. You may want to consider herbs, vegetables, flowers and so on.

Place the moss in a container with a small amount of potting soil. Transplant one or more plants into each container and hang from a strong hook in a sunny location. Water regularly and provide necessary nutrients. You may wish to hang these outside your house or in some nearby trees. Observe any animals that come to visit your hanging gardens.

Liana Vines

Lianas are climbing vines—twisting and drooping down from almost every tree in the rainforest. Typically, these vines begin as small seeds scattered about the forest floor. They quickly begin to sprout and climb their way up the trunk of a nearby tree. They often grow to lengths of 3,000 feet as they creep up the side of one tree, down another and back up the side of yet another. In many ways, they form a complicated web that links together much of the plant life of the rainforest.

Liana vines are incredibly strong and have been used to construct bridges across rivers and streams. They are also the source for rattan, a fiber used in the manufacture of selected types of furniture and baskets.

Liana vines—particularly their leaves—are a good example of how rainforest plants have adapted to this distinctive environment. Because so much rain falls in the forest, the leaves of many plants are constantly wet. The weight of the water and the dampness, which normally promote the growth of mold and fungi, could be disastrous for a plant. Many rainforest plants have "drip tips" or leaves that are shaped so that water quickly drains from their surfaces. You can see this in the following activity.

Drip, Drip, Drip

Collect samples of several different leaves from around your house or neighborhood. Tape each along the side of a piece of cardboard as in the illustration.

Place the cardboard across the top of a large cake pan and lean it at approximately a 45° angle. Use a medicine dropper and place one or two drops of water at the top of each leaf. Note the amount of time it takes for the drop(s) to roll down the surface of the leaves and fall into the pan. How does the shape of the leaf affect the speed of the water drops? Do any of the leaves have "drip tips"? How are those leaves similar to the leaves of rainforest plants?

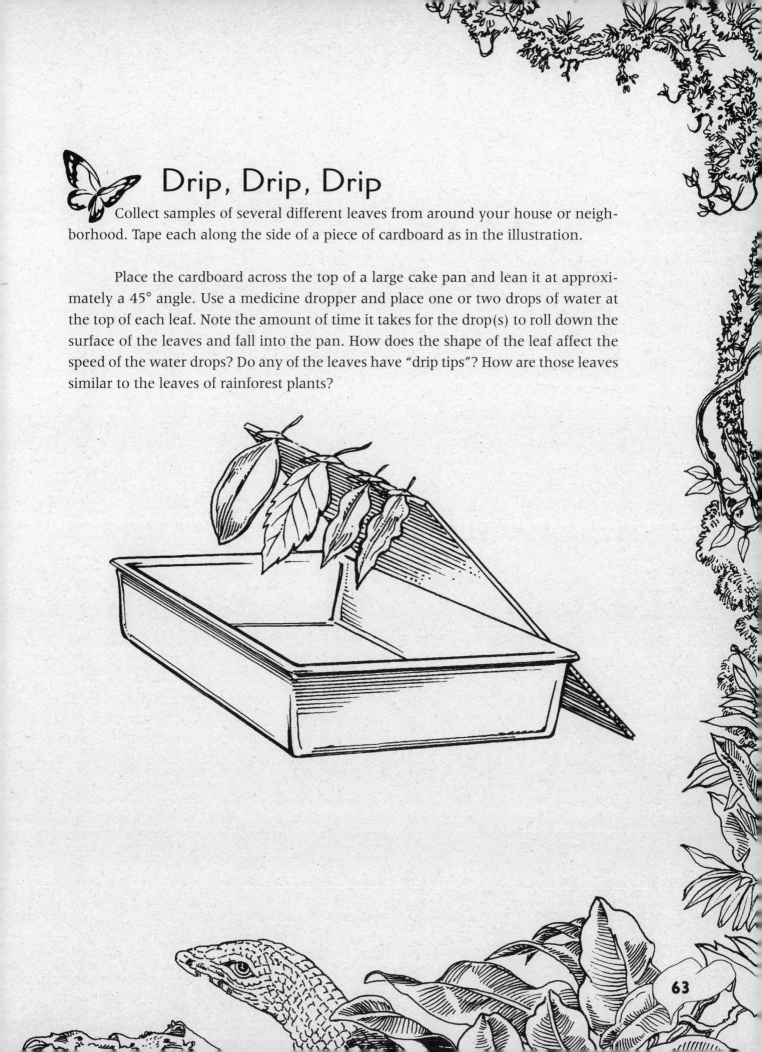

Strangler Fig

Natives of the rainforest often refer to this plant as the "tree killer." These plants can be found in many rainforests of the world, primarily in Central and South America.

Typically, the seeds of the strangler fig are deposited along the sides of another tree by birds and other animals. The seeds sprout and roots curl down toward the ground and into the soil. Long shoots are sent up that wrap around the trunk of the host tree. The shoots grow so large they choke off the tree's circulation. The fig's leaves are so large that sunlight is prevented from reaching any part of the host tree. Eventually, the host tree dies leaving the strangler fig in the shape of its now-dead host. The host tree eventually decomposes, and its circular shape is marked by the tangled vines of the strangler fig.

Although the strangler fig may seem to be a "cruel" plant, it actually serves a very useful purpose for animals living in the canopy. Its fruits are favored by monkeys and other tree-dwelling creatures.

Life in the canopy is hectic and busy. It's also filled with a wondrous array of plants and animals to be found nowhere else—either in the rainforest itself or in the entire world.

The Emergent Layer

Soaring up and beyond the thick canopy layer is the last, or fourth, layer of the rainforest. The emergent layer encompasses the crowns or heads of the tallest trees—trees reaching heights of 200 feet or more. In fact, if you could look at the rainforest from a helicopter, you might imagine that the emergent trees were a series of umbrellas popping up through breaks in the lush foliage of the rainforest.

Emergent trees are soaked in sunlight during the day and receive all of the rain that falls in the forest during the wet season. The leaves of emergent trees tend to be tough and leathery in order to reduce the amount of water that evaporates from them.

It is here that the majestic harpy eagle builds its nest and searches the layers below for a tasty snack or meal for its young. Colorful birds and many butterflies can also be found in the branches of these rainforest giants.

The Emergent Layer Checklist

▲ The tops of trees rise to heights of 250 feet.

▲ Nests of hawks, eagles and other birds of prey can be found.

▲ There are one or two emergent trees per acre of rainforest (on the average).

▲ More than 20 percent of the world's bird population lives in the emergent layer of the rainforest.

▲ Seeds from the trees are frequently light enough to be carried great distances by the wind.

▲ Slender tree trunks are supported by buttresses.

The emergent layer contains the tops of the tallest trees in the rainforest. Filled with a variety of animal life (primarily birds and butterflies), these trees are sparsely scattered throughout the entire forest. Because they are so tall, they are able to get sufficient sunlight and rainfall, necessary "ingredients" in the growth process.

As massive as these trees are in life, they also serve a useful purpose in death. When these towering giants die—either from old age, disease or lightning damage—they crash to the forest floor with a tremendous roar. As they fall they topple other trees, pulling down some with the spaghettilike web of vines that encircle all the rainforest trees. As a result, a patch of sunlight is able to break through the canopy layer and down into the understory or even the forest floor. Other plants take advantage of this additional sunlight and grow quite rapidly. Some of them may even have sufficient sunlight and other nutrients to grow into emergent trees.

Another benefit these trees provide in dying is through the nutrients they release into the soil as they decompose. The decomposition process is hastened by the millions of insects, bacteria and other organisms that thrive on the decaying trees. Even in death, the tree is able to provide and sustain life for a host of other organisms. This is a continuous process, one that takes place every day and one that has taken place for thousands of years.

My Adopted Tree

Emergent trees are an important part of the rainforest. Although you may not have any giant trees in your backyard or nearby park, you can learn a great deal about the trees (specifically, one tree) in your area through the following activity.

You'll need:

>   a camera
>   measuring tape
>   journal
>   plastic sandwich bags
>   string
>   a crayon
>   drawing paper

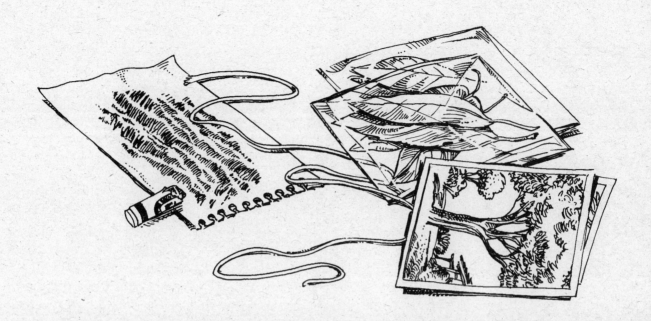

1. Locate a tree near where you live. If possible, select a deciduous tree (a tree that sheds its leaves each year). The tree should be in a location that's easy to reach, because you will be visiting your tree for the next 12 months.

2. Draw a picture of your tree (or take a photograph) and note any unusual markings, characteristics or patterns.

3. Measure 3 feet up the tree from the ground and wrap a piece of string around the tree at that point. Measure the string to determine the circumference of the tree.

4. Collect some of the tree's leaves and save them in plastic sandwich bags.

5. Place a piece of paper against the bark of the tree and rub a crayon over the paper until the bark pattern appears.

6. What other kinds of activities can you do with your "adopted" tree?

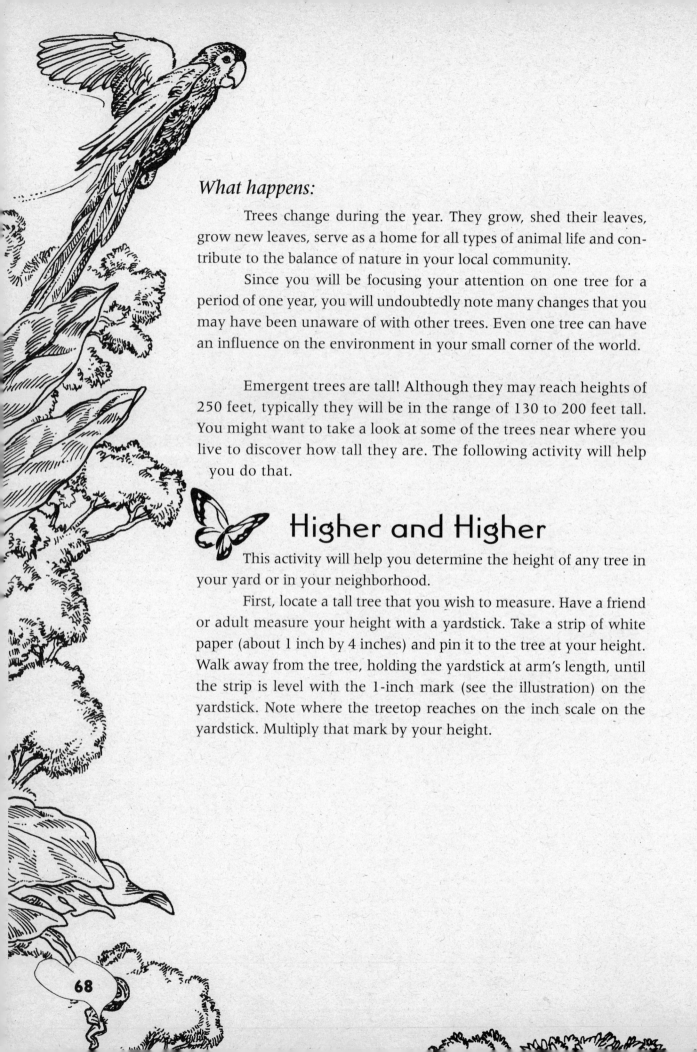

What happens:

Trees change during the year. They grow, shed their leaves, grow new leaves, serve as a home for all types of animal life and contribute to the balance of nature in your local community.

Since you will be focusing your attention on one tree for a period of one year, you will undoubtedly note many changes that you may have been unaware of with other trees. Even one tree can have an influence on the environment in your small corner of the world.

Emergent trees are tall! Although they may reach heights of 250 feet, typically they will be in the range of 130 to 200 feet tall. You might want to take a look at some of the trees near where you live to discover how tall they are. The following activity will help you do that.

Higher and Higher

This activity will help you determine the height of any tree in your yard or in your neighborhood.

First, locate a tall tree that you wish to measure. Have a friend or adult measure your height with a yardstick. Take a strip of white paper (about 1 inch by 4 inches) and pin it to the tree at your height. Walk away from the tree, holding the yardstick at arm's length, until the strip is level with the 1-inch mark (see the illustration) on the yardstick. Note where the treetop reaches on the inch scale on the yardstick. Multiply that mark by your height.

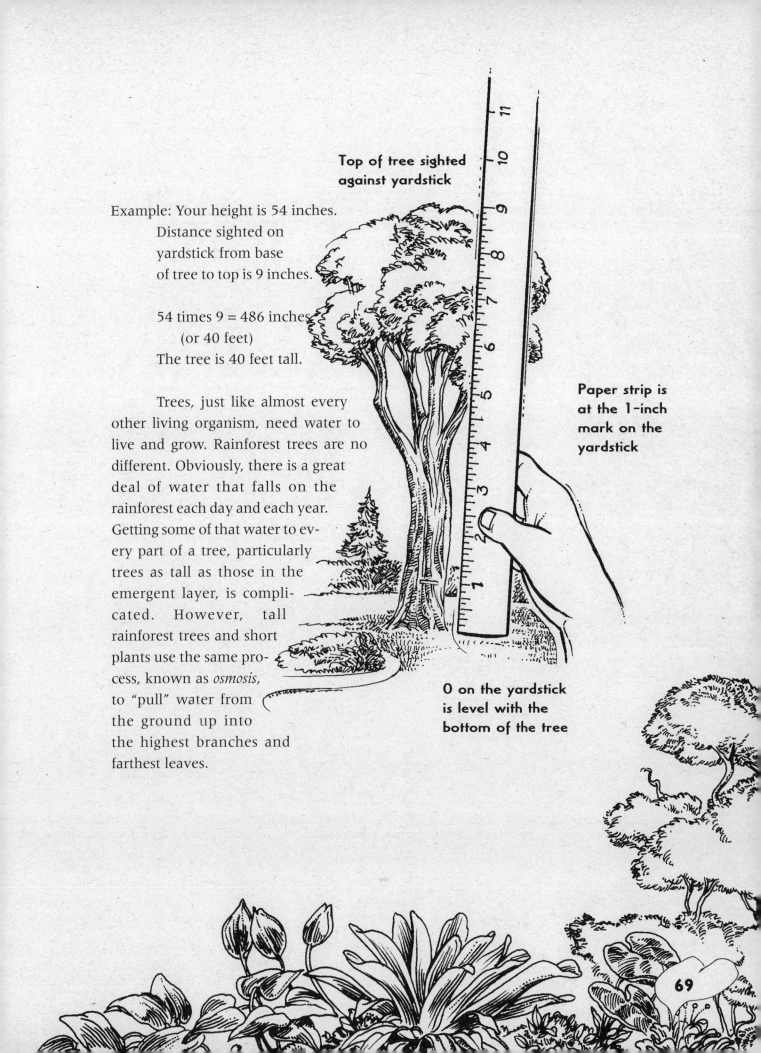

Top of tree sighted against yardstick

Example: Your height is 54 inches. Distance sighted on yardstick from base of tree to top is 9 inches.

54 times 9 = 486 inches
    (or 40 feet)
The tree is 40 feet tall.

Trees, just like almost every other living organism, need water to live and grow. Rainforest trees are no different. Obviously, there is a great deal of water that falls on the rainforest each day and each year. Getting some of that water to every part of a tree, particularly trees as tall as those in the emergent layer, is complicated. However, tall rainforest trees and short plants use the same process, known as *osmosis*, to "pull" water from the ground up into the highest branches and farthest leaves.

Paper strip is at the 1-inch mark on the yardstick

0 on the yardstick is level with the bottom of the tree

Going Up!

To survive, plants need to take in water from the ground and "transport" it to their limbs, branches and leaves. You can see this process in detail with the following activity. Take a leafy green stalk of celery and cut off some of the end. Place it in a glass of water that has been dyed with a few drops of food coloring. Leave it overnight and the next day notice how the colored water has risen up the celery stalk. Cut off a piece of the stalk and notice the colored tubes.

For an interesting variation, obtain one or two white carnations from a nearby florist. Place two glasses of water side by side and drop a few drops of one color of food coloring in one glass and a few drops of a different color of food coloring in another glass. Split the carnations up the stem and place one part of the stem in one glass and the other part of the stem in the other glass. Observe what happens after a few days. Notice how the colors have been "pulled" up into the flower. This process, osmosis, happens all the time in the plant world. It is how plants obtain the water and nutrients they need to survive.

The stems and roots of plants are not only important in "transporting" water and nutrients to all parts of a plant, they are equally important in providing support for the plant as well. Since the soil of the rainforest is so thin, the roots of the emergent trees must be strong to support their enormous weight. One adaptation that these giants have is known as *buttresses*, roots that grow out from the side of the main trunk and above the ground. If you were to look at one of these trees from the side, it would look as though the buttresses were an enormous dress radiating out from the base of the tree.

Although buttresses appear in other trees throughout the world, they are most common in the trees of the rainforest. Supporting the weight of a large tree and obtaining necessary nutrients are the primary functions of these "swirling" roots.

Support Structure

The following activity will help you understand the role of buttresses in the survival of a large rainforest tree.

You'll need:

>   an empty coffee can
>   sand
>   a long-stemmed carnation
>   2 stickpins
>   4 straws

1. Fill the coffee can with dry sand about three-quarters full.
2. Stick the carnation about 2 inches into the sand. Let go and notice how the carnation is unable to support itself. This is primarily due to the lack of a sufficient root system.

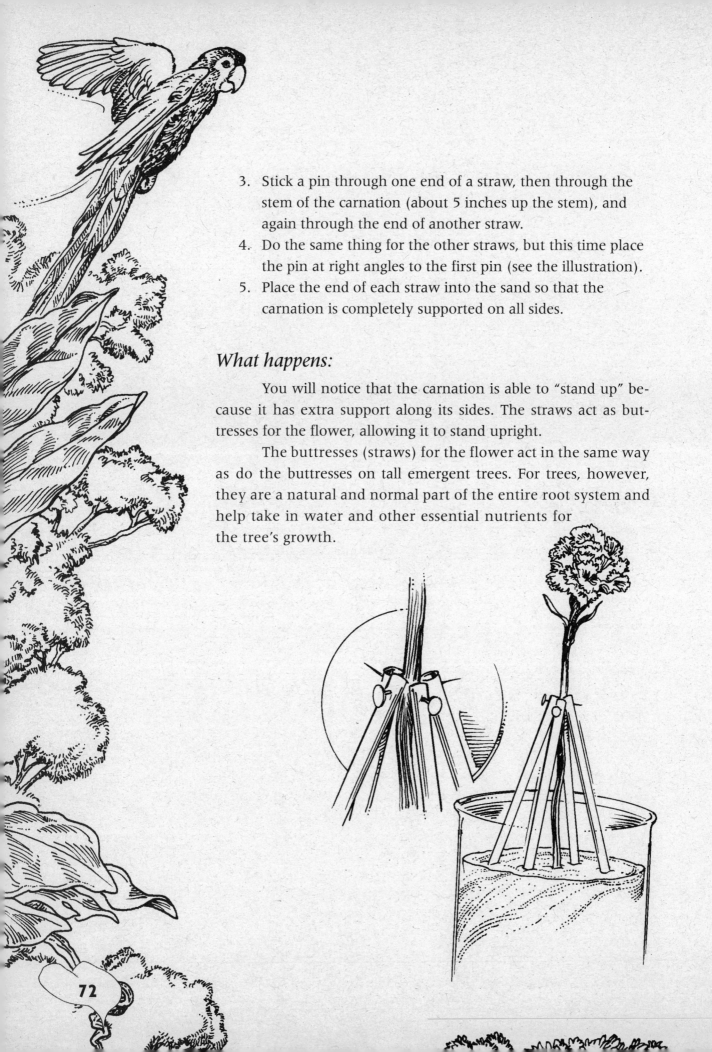

3. Stick a pin through one end of a straw, then through the stem of the carnation (about 5 inches up the stem), and again through the end of another straw.
4. Do the same thing for the other straws, but this time place the pin at right angles to the first pin (see the illustration).
5. Place the end of each straw into the sand so that the carnation is completely supported on all sides.

What happens:

You will notice that the carnation is able to "stand up" because it has extra support along its sides. The straws act as buttresses for the flower, allowing it to stand upright.

The buttresses (straws) for the flower act in the same way as do the buttresses on tall emergent trees. For trees, however, they are a natural and normal part of the entire root system and help take in water and other essential nutrients for the tree's growth.

Bird-Watching

The emergent layer is filled with birds—thousands and thousands of birds. The swoop of a "dive-bombing" harpy eagle, the shrill cry of an distant macaw and the whir of a hummingbird's wings keep this part of the rainforest alive and active. Thousands of nests are found, not only in the emergent tress but in the canopy below. As a result, the top two layers of the rainforest often seem to be a bird-watchers' paradise.

Here are just a few of the birds you might find in the emergent layer:

Amazon hummingbirds	anhingas
flycatchers	forest falcons
harpy eagles	honey guides
jacanas	jackamars
jacobins	king vultures
macaws	oropendolas
parrots	quetzales
tanagers	toucans
vultures	weaverbirds

Bird-watching can be an exciting and enjoyable hobby. You may be surprised at the wide variety of birds in your own region of the country or just in your own backyard. Perhaps you'd like to construct some birdhouses to attract a variety of birds to your house.

For easy and inexpensive ideas on making your own birdhouses, write to the National Wildlife Federation (1400 16th Street, NW, Washington, DC 20036 [202] 797-6800) and ask for a free copy of *Recycle for the Birds*. If you're interested in learning more about the birds in your area, get a copy of the book *A Kid's First Book of Bird-watching* published by The National Audubon Society (666 Pennsylvania Avenue, SE, Washington, DC 20003 [202] 547-9009). This book, with an accompanying cassette tape, can be found in many larger bookstores.

Bountiful Butterflies

The emergent layer is also filled with an enormous variety of butterflies. In fact, some of the most beautiful butterflies to be found anywhere can usually be located high up in the emergent or canopy layers of the world's rainforests.

You may be interested in investigating the butterflies in your area of the country or raising your own. The following products are all available from Delta Education (P.O. Box 3000, Nashua, NH 03061-3000; [800] 442-5444):

- Butterfly Tower (catalog #53-021-2288): Watch the growth and development of your own butterflies right at home. The tower is 6 feet by 14 inches and includes overlapping netting to allow easy access for feeding. It also includes complete instructions and a coupon for five painted lady butterfly larvae.

- Butterfly Garden (catalog #53-020-6007): This kit includes a butterfly chamber, instructions and a coupon for butterfly larvae. It is appropriate for use indoors.

- Butterfly Feeder (catalog #53-060-3877): This feeder will attract many butterflies in the local area. The feeder can be hung from a tree branch or mounted on a post.

The tall green "umbrellas" of the emergent layer hold a variety of species and a variety of surprises. An important part of the life of the rainforest, the trees are home to plants and animals to be found in no other location on the face of the earth. Always exciting and frequently mysterious, these organisms are at the "top" of the rainforest, yet are intricately woven into the fabric of daily rainforest life.

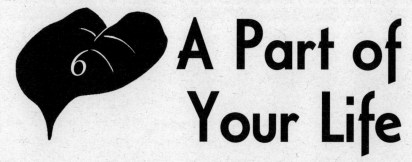

A Part of Your Life

You may be wondering why you should be interested in a place that is hundreds or thousands of miles away from where you live. Why should you be interested in a part of the world you may never see or visit. What does the rainforest have to do with you? These are good questions, and the answer is that the rainforest is a part of your life.

When you breathe, the rainforest is contributing to your breathing. When you eat dinner, the rainforest may be contributing to the foods or spices you find on your plate. When you go to the store, some of the products you buy may come from the rainforest or be manufactured by people who live in the rainforest. When you get sick, a medicine prescribed by your doctor may have its origins in the rainforest. Indeed, the rainforest may be contributing more to your daily life than you might imagine. Let's take a look at how the rainforest touches your life.

Climate

Even though you may live thousands of miles away from the nearest rainforest, that part of the world may have a lot to do with the type of climate (weather over a long period of time) you experience where you live. Indeed, many scientists believe that rainforests are a significant factor in the climate of the entire planet.

When you breathe, you take in oxygen and give off carbon dioxide. In fact, all animals give off carbon dioxide. On the other hand, that carbon dioxide is used by all green plants to make food. Without carbon dioxide, plants would not be able to survive; without the oxygen produced by plants, animals would not be able to survive. As you can see plants and animals need each other.

Due to modern technology, however, people have put more and more carbon dioxide into the air. This CO_2 (the symbol for carbon dioxide) is produced by cars, trucks and factories. In fact, tons and tons of additional CO_2 is added to the atmosphere each and every year. As that CO_2 rises into the atmosphere, it traps extra heat near the earth's surface. That extra heat causes the earth to warm more than it would otherwise. This effect is known to scientists as the Greenhouse Effect, where the entire planet is turned into a greenhouse, much like one you might find in someone's garden.

If the earth continues to warm up, some scientists speculate that over the next few centuries the climate in many places would change dramatically. Summers would be longer; some crops would not be able to grow; violent storms would affect many parts of the planet and ice-covered areas of the earth would melt, resulting in rising sea levels.

Green plants, such as those in the world's rainforest, are needed to absorb the quantities of CO_2 released into the air. However, if these rainforests are destroyed, there are fewer plants available to absorb the CO_2. If humans continue to put more and more CO_2 into the atmosphere while, at the same time, destroying vast sections of rainforest, we may see some significant and unexpected changes in the world's climate. In short, the world's rainforests are important in maintaining the world's climate.

Food and Other Products

If you have ever been in a grocery store you know the wide variety of food available there. Food in brightly colored packages, food displayed on racks and counters and food in large oversized freezers … all available for us to eat just by picking them up and placing them in a shopping cart.

What we may sometimes forget is that all that food had to begin somewhere, either as part of a plant or part of an animal. (This excludes artificially created foods that originated in a laboratory.) In fact, if you have ever eaten a chocolate bar, a pineapple, a tomato or a banana, you've eaten a food product that originated in the rainforest. Many of the food products we take for granted have their origins in the jungles of the rainforest. Because so many people drink coffee, tea and hot chocolate, and eat oranges, grapefruit, pineapples and sugar for breakfast, one scientist stated, "Each and every one of us is eating tropical rainforests for breakfast."

Around the House

If you look around your house you may discover a host of rainforest products. Here's a list of some of the raw materials obtained from the rainforest and used in many home products:

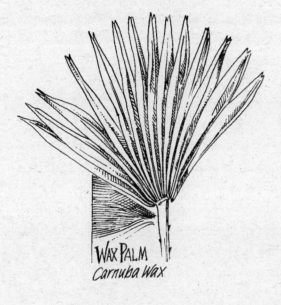

WAX PALM
Carnuba Wax

acids	alcohols
balsa wood	bamboo
camphor	chicle
citronella	dyes
fibers	flavorings
hemp	kapok
latexes	mahogany
oils	palms
rattan	resins
rubber	spices
sweeteners	teak
waxes	

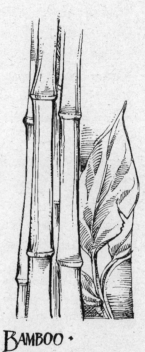

BAMBOO •

What are some of the items in your home made from these raw materials?

Medicines

According to many scientists, the rainforest is a rich treasure trove of potential medicines just waiting to be discovered. Some experts estimate that only about 1 percent of all the potential medicines that might come from the rainforest have been discovered. That means that a vast storehouse of medicines and drugs lie undiscovered in the depths of the world's rainforests.

One of the ways in which scientists are learning about the healing properties of rainforest plants is by talking with the indigenous peoples of the rainforest. This branch of science, known as ethnobotony, or the study of traditional uses of plants by native peoples, has yielded an incredible array of potentially lifesaving drugs. For thousands of years, people of the rainforest have been using plants to cure diseases and heal different illnesses. For example, natives have used rainforest plants to treat illnesses such as arthritis and to heal snake bites and skin infections. Rainforest people have discovered the marvelous and miraculous cures available right in their own "backyard" and are sharing some of that knowledge with doctors and researchers from around the world.

Some people have called the rainforest the world's medicine chest because of its potential for curing diseases such as cancer, AIDS and influenza. In fact, fully two-thirds of all the medicines people use today have their origins in rainforest plants.

One of the reasons why there are so many potential medicines "locked" in the rainforest is simply because there is such a wide variety of plants there. Many of those plants have developed chemicals or poisons which help protect them from being eaten by insects and other animals. While those chemicals may be distasteful or deadly to rainforest animals, they may be quite helpful to humans in curing specific diseases or treating life-threatening illnesses.

When you obtain medicines from your local pharmacy, there is a one in five chance that the ingredient(s) originated from a plant native to the rainforest. Ask your parents if you can look in the family medicine cabinet for hydrocortisone (used to treat rashes, itches and inflammation) and ipecac (used to induce vomiting in cases of accidental poisoning).

Ask to speak to your family doctor or pharmacist about rainforest drugs used in the treatment of the following diseases and illnesses:

Disease	Medicine
malaria	quinine
nervous disorders	reserpine
leukemia	vincristine
heart disease	digitalis
tetanus	curare
arthritis	cortison
leukemia, Hodgkin's disease and various cancers	drugs from the rosy periwinkle plant

Biodiversity

The rainforests of the world contain an incredible diversity of plant and animal life. As you learned earlier, more than 50 percent of all the species of plants and animals can be found in the rainforest. Imagine if all those organisms were eliminated. Compare it to eliminating half of all the libraries or half of all the books in the world!

Many scientists are worried that whole species of plants and animals are being eliminated from the world's rainforests even before they are discovered and classified. Calculations by several scientists estimate that there may be between 5 and 10 million species of plants and animals in the rainforests of the world. One scientist has even estimated that rainforests may contain as many as 30 million species of insects alone! Although scientists may never agree on the exact number of plants and animals in the rainforest, they all agree that there are more species in this particular ecosystem than in all the other ecosystems of the world combined.

All of these plants and animals represent the incredible variety of life on the planet. So, too, is this variety woven together in a complex web of survival that many scientists are only beginning to understand. Equally important is the fact that many of the products we depend on are possible because of this intricate and complex array of plants and animals. Indeed, if many of them were eliminated from the face of the earth, many of the substances and products we need for our daily (or future) living might also be eliminated.

While the richest biodiversity of organisms exists in the world's rainforests, there is also a marvelous biodiversity of plants and animals in your part of the world, too. The following activities will help you learn about and appreciate the species with whom you live each day.

Water World

Here's how you can construct a simple and inexpensive ecosystem (an aquarium) in your own home.

You'll need:

 a large commercial mayonnaise jar (You can obtain one from your school cafeteria
   or have your parents purchase one from a large supermarket.)
gravel
sand
aquatic plants
guppies or goldfish
water snails
wire screen

1. Thoroughly wash and rinse out the mayonnaise jar.
2. Wash and rinse the gravel and sand. (You can purchase washed sand at an aquarium store.) Place a 1-inch layer of gravel and a 1-inch layer of sand on the bottom of the jar.
3. Fill the jar almost to the top with tap water and allow the jar to sit undisturbed for 48 hours. This allows the chlorine in the water to evaporate.

4. Obtain 2 or 3 aquatic plants (such as elodea plants) from an aquarium store and place them in the bottom of the jar. Make sure they are firmly rooted in the sand.

5. Place 2 or 3 goldfish and 2 or 3 snails in the jar. Place a piece of wire screening over the top of the jar.

What happens:

This miniature ecosystem will be able to sustain itself for several weeks. To make sure your ecosystem will work for a longer time, obtain an inexpensive air pump for your aquarium. Be sure to feed the fish some fish food occasionally. Plants and animals need each other to survive. In an aquatic environment, such as your aquarium, the plants provide necessary oxygen for the fish and snails.

The fish provide nourishment (with their wastes) for the plants and for the eventual growth of smaller plants such as algae. The algae serve as a food source for the snails. When properly maintained, this miniature ecosystem will be "in balance."

Photo Opportunity

Obtain an inexpensive camera and several rolls of film. Take a walking tour around your neighborhood or community. Use the camera to take photographs of all the animals you find. You'll probably note some on the ground, others in the plants and trees, a few in the air and perhaps others in pools, puddles, streams or nearby lakes. Be sure to search for, and take pictures of, as many different types of animals as you can. When the photos are developed arrange them into a photo album by category (Mammals, Fish, Insects, Birds, Reptiles, Amphibians, I Don't Know).

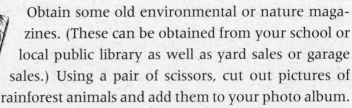

Obtain some old environmental or nature magazines. (These can be obtained from your school or local public library as well as yard sales or garage sales.) Using a pair of scissors, cut out pictures of rainforest animals and add them to your photo album. What kinds of similarities, for example, do you note between mammals of the rainforest and mammals in your neighborhood? How about insects or birds?

If you like, create a separate photo album of neighborhood plants and rainforest plants.

Avian Café

Watching birds can be an enjoyable hobby that can last a lifetime. Obtain an inexpensive pair of binoculars (the 8 by 30 size is recommended), a notebook, a pen and colored pencils, a small tape recorder and a field guide to help you identify the birds.

Here's an easy-to-make bird feeder that will help attract birds to your house: Use a scrap piece of lumber approximately 15 inches by 15 inches. (You may want to vary the dimensions.) Nail or glue thin strips of wood along the four sides, leaving gaps at all four corners for water drainage. Nail this platform to a post or pole and place it in the ground so that the platform is approximately 5 feet above ground level. If you wish, you may want to attach some lightweight chains to all four corners of the platform and hang your feeder in a nearby tree. Sprinkle the surface of the platform with a thin layer of birdseed or sunflower seeds. Check the feeder regularly to clean off any shells and to add new food.

Use your notebook to record the types and numbers of birds that visit your feeder. You may also wish to experiment with different types of bird food and note the different types of birds that visit the feeder.

You'll probably discover that birds are most active in the spring and early summer as well as in the early fall. The best time to see birds is just before dawn or just before dusk: birds are least active during midday.

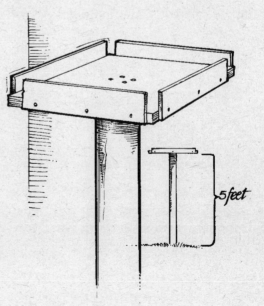

5 feet

When bird-watching, move carefully and slowly. Remain still whenever possible. Note any activity in the sky, trees and bushes, or on the ground. Carefully note the varieties of birds in your area. Obtain a field guide from your local library or bookstore and use it to identify the specific features of each bird. Details can be recorded in your notebook and an illustration can be prepared with the colored pencils. Be sure to take your bird-watching equipment with you when you travel and note the different types of birds in areas away from where you live.

Stamp Study

You may wish to start a stamp collection that concentrates on the plants and animals of the rainforest. Many tropical countries issue stamps depicting the indigenous flora and fauna of their native land. Visit a local hobby store or stamp store and ask about stamps from tropical countries. You can buy an inexpensive stamp album to house your collection. Stamp collecting is a wonderful way to learn about the plants and animals of the world as well as about the countries from which they come.

As you can see, the rainforest is a natural and regular part of your everyday life. Making sure that it is still around will ensure that the products we obtain from the rainforest will be constantly available. It's up to all of us—working together—to preserve this valuable and necessary ecosystem.

A Disappearing World

Think about this: Every year the world loses an area of tropical rainforest the size of the state of Washington. That means that all the trees, all the monkeys, all the birds and caterpillars, all the lizards, frogs, liana vines and bromeliads are wiped out … gone … destroyed, never to return again. Some scientists predict that by the year 2050 all the rainforests of the world will have vanished for good.

Gone, too, will be all the plants and animals of the rainforest. For the people who live in the rainforest and who depend on those plants and animals, this means that their foods and crops may also be eliminated. Imagine going to your local grocery store one day and finding that it's no longer there, and all the other grocery stores for miles around have disappeared, too. You would find it difficult to find the things you needed to survive, just as the people of the rainforest would find it difficult to survive if all plants and animals were wiped out.

Your Town

Think about your town. Now imagine that you wake up one morning and all of the following events had occurred:

1. Half of all the animals (dogs, cats, birds and so on) in your town had disappeared.
2. Eighty percent of the fruits, vegetables, breads and cereals in all of the grocery stores had simply vanished.
3. All of the rope, hardware, ladders and tools in all the hardware stores in town had disappeared.
4. All of the wood, timber and lumber in town had been collected in a large pile and was being burned.

83

How would you feel? Would you be able to get enough to eat, find sufficient materials to build a home or locate materials to plant a garden? Would you be able to survive? It would be difficult, if not impossible, to survive. Now you have some idea of how the indigenous peoples of the rainforest feel when large sections of their habitat are destroyed.

As a scientist you might ask, "Why is rainforest land being destroyed, and why are many plants and animals being eliminated?" The answers are both simple and complex. Let's take a look at some of the major causes:

1. The rainforest is a valuable storehouse of trees and lumber. Many countries around the world have limited lumber resources. As a result, these countries often turn to rainforest countries to supply their timber needs.

2. As you know, rainforest soil is poor in nutrients. However, people need to grow crops to survive. When they do that, the meager nutrients in the soil are soon exhausted. In two or three years, families need to move to other sections of the rainforest, clear and burn the surrounding vegetation and begin to grow more crops. This cycle continues throughout the world's rainforests. (Note: When trees and other plants are eliminated, so, too, are the homes and habitats of many rainforest animals.)

3. In certain rainforest countries cattle ranchers frequently clear away large sections of land by chopping and burning trees. Cattle are released to graze in those deforested areas. The nutrient-poor soil cannot support the nutritional needs of cattle for very long and more land needs to be cleared away.

4. As the world's population grows so does that of the world's cities and towns. These municipalities need more space to expand. As the cities grow, land is cleared away. In many of the tropical countries of the world, much of that clearing takes place along the edges of the rainforest. In other words, as a population increases, rainforest land often decreases.

5. Many of the world's rainforests are located in financially poor countries that need to borrow money from wealthier countries, such as the United States. The people in those countries are encouraged to harvest the resources of the rainforest and to sell those products around the world. The money received from these sales is used to pay off the debts. To keep paying those debts, more and more rainforest land needs to be cleared away.

6. The rainforest is an area rich in natural resources. In some South American countries, vast deposits of valuable minerals, such as gold and mercury, have been discovered on rainforest land. Mining companies often clear away large sections of the rainforest to obtain these resources.

7. In many rainforest countries, developers working for private businesses or governments construct dams, roads, logging trails, small businesses and towns throughout this ecosystem. Unfortunately, a lot of this construction is poorly planned, poorly developed and poorly maintained. The result is more rainforest acreage that is permanently destroyed.

Running Away

Here's an activity that will illustrate the speed with which soil nutrients can be depleted in just a short amount of time.

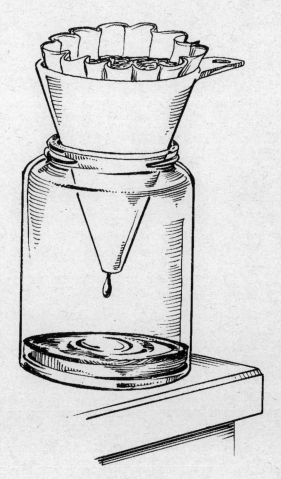

You'll need:

    blue tempera paint (available at most hobby
        or art supply stores)
    dry dirt
    funnel
    a large, wide-mouth jar
    coffee filters
    water

1. Add 1/4 teaspoon dry blue tempera paint to 1/2 cup dry dirt and mix thoroughly.
2. Set a funnel in a large, wide-mouth jar and place a coffee filter in the funnel.
3. Pour the soil mixture into the filter.
4. Pour 1/2 cup water into the funnel and note the color of the water running into the jar. Pour off the water in the jar, put the funnel over the jar again, and repeat this again with another 1/2 cup water. Pour off the water and repeat another 2 or 3 times.

What happens:

You'll probably note that the water flowing into the jar the first time will be dark blue in color. Each time the experiment is repeated (with the same mixture of soil) the color will become progressively lighter. Eventually, the water will run clean into the jar. The blue tempera paint represents the nutrients that naturally occur in the soil. These nutrients are necessary for plants to grow. Whenever there is a lot of rain or water runoff, however, the water takes away these nutrients, leaving behind nutrient-poor soil. Excessive rain or runoff can deplete the soil of valuable materials needed for plant growth. If large quantities of rainforest plants are removed or eliminated from an area, then the soil (and its nutrients) cannot be held in place. Subsequent rains will quickly deplete the soil of necessary nutrients. As more and more rainforest trees and plants are cut down, more and more soil nutrients are washed away.

Strong Grass

The following experiment will help you see how important plant life is to the natural ecology of the rainforest.

You'll need:

2 rectangular cake pans (9 inches by 13 inches)
grass seed
soil
water
a brick or heavy book

1. Fill both of the rectangular cake pans with soil. In the first pan, sprinkle some grass seed on the surface, press into the soil, and water thoroughly. Don't plant any grass in the second pan.
2. After the grass in the first pan has reached a height of 2 to 3 inches, place the end of each pan on a book or brick so that they are both at an angle.
3. Fill a pitcher with water and pour it at the top of the first pan (the one with grass). Do the same thing with the pan that just has dirt in it.

What happens:

You'll notice that the pan without the grass allows the water to flow freely across its surface. You may even note that some of the dirt is carried toward the bottom of the pan. In the other pan, the grass slows down the flow of the water and prevents the soil from washing away. In other words, the vegetation (grass) in the pan retards or slows down the rate of erosion. When trees and plants are eliminated in a particular area, erosion can become a serious problem.

All of the previously listed events, in differing degrees and in different combinations, are contributing to the destruction, deforestation and elimination of vast sections of rainforest land. Working to save the rainforests of the world means working on all of these problems together.

Conservation Efforts

There's no question that the rainforests of the world are in serious danger. It's not easy to erase hundreds of years of abuse to the rainforest. Many organizations, environmental groups and local governments are working hard to reduce, slow down or eliminate some of these problems. Let's take a look at some of the worldwide efforts being employed by governments and people just like you to preserve the dwindling rainforests of the world.

People Power

Perhaps the best way to preserve the rainforests of the world is when people get together to address an issue, write to their government officials and raise money to assist these endangered regions of the world. There is a wide variety of groups and organizations around the world working to preserve this dwindling ecosystem.

While groups and organizations can do much to assist preservation efforts, individuals can make a difference too. Many people working alone have written and visited government officials, worked with the indigenous people of the rainforest and contributed money toward important conservation projects. You, too, can be a factor in the conservation and preservation of the rainforest (see chapter 8.

Working Together

You and your friends may want to organize a Rainforest Club in your local area. Your club can be dedicated to informing people about the destruction of the world's rainforests, or it can arrange a series of fund-raising projects in which the money collected can be sent to a group or organization dedicated to preserving the rainforest. Members of the club can volunteer to help a local environmental group in their efforts to save the rainforest. For additional ideas on what your club can do see chapter 8.

Setting Land Aside

Several governments (most notably in South America) have set aside large tracts of land as *reserves,* which means that these parcels of land cannot be developed or destroyed. They are preserved for the native peoples, plants and animals that live there. Nonnative people may not settle or build in these areas.

Several of these reserves have been designated as *extractive reserves,* large areas in which the native people can extract (or collect) natural products from the forest. These products may include latex (used in the manufacture of rubber products), chicle (used in the manufacture of chewing gum), fruits and nuts. These reserves are safe-guarded by government agencies and strict environmental laws. Monies from conservation groups in the United States are also used in helping to set aside extractive reserves.

More or Less

Take three small milk cartons and fill each three-quarters full with soil. Plant the first carton with a little birdseed, the second with a moderate amount of birdseed and the third with a lot of birdseed. Be sure to vary the amount of seed in each carton. Water regularly and watch as the seeds sprout. Notice what happens in each of the cartons. Evaluate the growth of plants in each carton. How much does overcrowding (in the third carton) contribute to and detract from the growth of all the plants? How does the growth rate in the third carton compare with the rate in the first carton?

Sustainable Development

The rainforests of the world represent a delicate balance in nature. They have existed for thousands of years, yet have suffered an incredible amount of destruction in just the past 200 years. One response to this problem is *sustainable development*, the harvesting of rainforest products over an extended period of time without significantly affecting the balance of nature.

For example, the growing and harvesting of Brazil nuts (a popular addition to mixed nuts and ice cream) provides a significant income for indigenous peoples of the rainforest, helps sustain them over long periods of time and does not require the cutting down or deforestation of large tracts of land. As a result, the government of Brazil has set aside several parcels of land for the production of Brazil nuts. In fact, this type of sustainable agriculture is generating four times more revenue than cattle grazing on the same amount of land.

Sustainable development not only has an economic benefit for rainforest countries, but also for the indigenous people who call the rainforest their home. Providing a source of income without sacrificing the environment is helping people continue to live and work on ancestral lands.

One company—Community Products, Inc.—believes the rainforest can be more profitable as a living sustainable resource. Each year it purchases more than 150 tons of Brazil nuts that are harvested wild from the rainforest. These nuts are used in the manufacture of products such as Rainforest Crunch, Rainforest Crunch Bar, Rainforest Chew Bar, Rainforest Truffles, Rainforest Crunch Popcorn, and Chocolate Covered Rainforest Crunch. Community Products believes that increased demand for these products will provide an economic incentive to keep the rainforest alive. The company also commits an amount equal to 60 percent of after-tax profits (more than $525,000) to nonprofit organizations striving to protect the rainforests of the world. Call or write Community Products for information on their products:

Community Products, Inc.
R.D. 2, Box 1950
Montpelier, VT 05602
(800) 927-2695

Ecotourism

Various definitions of the term *ecotourism* abound, although it is most commonly used to describe any recreation or vacation in a natural environment. The Ecotourism Society defines ecotourism as "purposeful travel to natural areas to understand the culture and natural history of the environment, taking care not to alter the integrity of the ecosystem, while producing economic opportunities that make the conservation of natural resources beneficial to local people." In other words, people can travel to other countries to view or explore the natural environment rather than visiting theme parks or just sightseeing.

It should be pointed out that ecotourism by itself does not significantly impact the preservation of the rainforest. It is the money spent by tourists in a rainforest area that can be used to help preserve sections of that environment. In short, the money visitors and tourists bring into a country are used to help preserve the natural environment of that country.

Many countries view ecotourism as an exciting new way to obtain the funds necessary for preservation efforts. Funds generated can be used for conservation, management and reforestation of valuable rainforest lands. Problems arise, however, if too many tourists are allowed into an area; the delicate balance of nature can be damaged or seriously altered.

All Aboard!

Visit or write travel agencies in your area. Obtain brochures, leaflets, pamphlets and other materials on travel in and to rainforest countries. Be sure to share this information with your classmates, teacher and parents. You may wish to assemble the information you obtain into an attractive notebook or three-ring binder.

Following are the addresses and telephone numbers of national tour agencies who regularly offer trips to rainforest countries. You may wish to contact them and ask about free brochures and other materials.

Adventure Source
1111 East Madison, Suite 302
Seattle, WA 98122
(800) 249-2885

Eco Expeditions
10629 North Kendall Drive
Miami, FL 33176
(800) 854-0023

Ecotour Expeditions, Inc.
P.O. Box 381066
Cambridge, MA 02238
(800) 688-1822

Geo Expeditions
P.O. Box 3656-A12
Sonora, CA 95370
(800) 351-5041

International Expeditions, Inc.
One Environs Park
Helena, AL 35080
(800) 633-4734

Questars Worldwide Nature Tours
257 Park Avenue South
New York, NY 10010
(800) 468-8668

Special Interest Tours
10220 North 27th Street
Phoenix, AZ 85028
(800) 525-6772

Preserving the rainforests of the world will take the combined efforts of many people, groups and governments. When we all work together for a common cause, however, much can be done to save this important and necessary ecosystem.

What You Can Do

The rainforests of the world are rich and valuable environments that are in danger. Trees are being cleared, animal species are being eliminated and populations of native peoples are being severely reduced. In a few decades, the inhabitants of the rainforest may be gone forever.

Many young people, such as yourself, are interested in preserving rainforests around the world. By joining together we can all work toward saving this valuable ecosystem. Although many rainforests are in danger of being severely destroyed or eradicated, there are things we can do today to help preserve what is left of the world's surviving rainforests.

Contact Environmental Groups

There are many environmental groups throughout the United States working to save and protect the rainforests of the world. These organizations not only produce films, brochures and other types of information for the public, but they also raise money to help purchase tracts of land, legislate for strict environmental laws and provide opportunities for people to visit rainforests and work with local inhabitants.

Perhaps you and your friends or classmates can contact several of these groups and ask for information on the work they do and the types of printed materials they have available for students. Several of these organizations have local groups in cities all across the United States. You may wish to contact the leaders of one or more of these local affiliates and learn about some of the programs and information they provide.

Children's Alliance for
Protection of the Environment (CAPE)
P.O. Box 307
Austin, TX 78767

Children's Rainforest
P.O. Box 936
Lewiston, ME 04240

Conservation International
1015 18th Street, NW, Suite 1000
Washington, DC 20036
(202) 429-5660

Cultural Survival
215 First Street
Cambridge, MA 02142
(617) 621-3818

Defenders of Wildlife
1244 19th Street, NW
Washington, DC 20036

Friends of the Earth
1025 Vermont Avenue, NW, Suite 300
Washington, DC 20005
(202) 783-7400

Friends of Wildlife Conservation
New York Zoological Society
185th Street, Southern Boulevard
Bronx Zoo
Bronx, NY 10460
(718) 220-5100

Marine World Africa USA
Marine World Parkway
Vallejo, CA 94589
(707) 644-4000

National Audubon Society
666 Pennsylvania Avenue, SE
Washington, DC 20003
(202) 547-9009

National Wildlife Federation
1400 16th Street, NW
Washington, DC 20036
(202) 797-6800

Natural Resources Defense Council
1350 New York Avenue, NW
Washington, DC 20005
(202) 783-7800

Nature Conservancy International
1815 North Lynn Street
Arlington, VA 22209
(703) 841-5300

Rainforest Action Network
450 Sansome Street, Suite 700
San Francisco, CA 94111
(415) 398-4404

Rainforest Alliance
65 Bleecker Street
New York, NY 10012-2420
(212) 677-1900

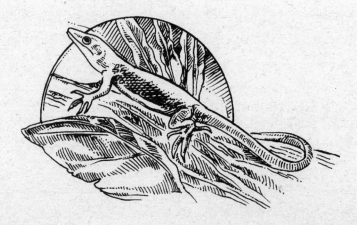

Rainforest Preservation Foundation
P.O. Box 820308
Fort Worth, TX 76182
(800) 460-RAIN

Save the Rainforest
604 Jamie Street
Dodgeville, WI 53533

Sierra Club
730 Polk Street
San Francisco, CA 94109
(415) 923-5660

Smithsonian Tropical Research Institute
Unit 0948
APO AA 34002-0948

Tree Amigos/Center for
Environmental Study
143 Bostwick NE
Grand Rapids, MI 49503
(616) 771-3935

Trees for the Future
11306 Estona Drive
P.O. Box 1786
Silver Spring, MD 20915-1786
(301) 929-0238

The Wilderness Society
1400 "I" Street, NW
Washington, DC 20005

World-Wide Fund for Nature
1250 24th Street, NW
Washington, DC 20037
(202) 293-4800

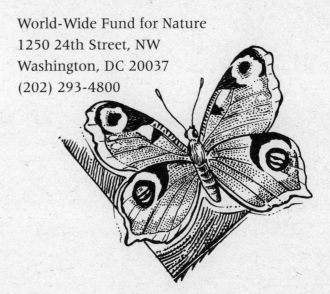

Write to Government Officials

One way you can help in the preservation of the world's rainforests is by writing letters to national and international government officials. This includes the senators and representatives from your state, the U.S. president and the leaders of foreign countries.

You and your friends may wish to start a letter-writing campaign and enlist your parents and relatives in doing the same. While you may not receive a reply to every one of these letters, you can be sure that they will be read. When government officials get many letters advocating a particular point of view, they pay attention. The "voice of the people" is very important in helping shape the policies and practices of any country. If many people care enough to write letters of concern, then necessary action may be taken.

If you would like to obtain the addresses of people around the world to whom you can send a letter, contact the folks at *P3, The Earth-Based Magazine for Kids* (P.O. Box 52, Montgomery, VT 05470). You might also want to inquire about subscribing to this terrific magazine.

Write to Other Students

You can enlist other students across the country and around the world in helping to preserve the rainforests. Following are the addresses of several agencies through which you can correspond with other students about various issues. You may wish to select a "pen pal" in a rainforest country and get firsthand information about what is happening in his or her homeland. Or you may want to write to someone in another country and find out what steps his or her government is taking to curb destruction of the rainforests.

Please be aware that some of the organizations listed below may require a fee for their services, so you might want to check with your parents before starting out. Perhaps your class or your school could get involved in writing letters to students from all over the world. What a wonderful way to share ideas, discuss problems, plan ideas and become informed about rainforest activities all over the earth!

Afro-Asian Center
P.O. Box 337
Saugerties, NY 12477

International Pen Pals
P.O. Box 2900065
Brooklyn, NY 11229-0001

Friends Forever School Network
P.O. Box 20103
Park West Station
New York, NY 10025

Student Letter Exchange
630 Third Avenue
New York, NY 10017

International Pen Friends
4510 West 67th Street
Prairie Village, KS 66208

Student Letter Exchange
215 Fifth Avenue
Wasecu, MN 56093

Know What You Buy

As you have learned in this book, there are many products obtained from the rainforest. Medicines and foods are just some of the items we use every day and upon which we depend. Without them our lives would be considerably different.

It's important to note that there are many rainforest products we can purchase. These items are obtained through a process known as *sustainability*—which is the harvesting or collection of rainforest products without degrading the various ecosystems of the forest. By purchasing sustainably harvested rainforest products, we can help prevent or slow down the elimination of valuable rainforest lands, while, at the same time, supporting the economies of the indigenous people living there. Certain food items and natural products can be harvested from the rainforests without destroying the environment. Buying these products encourages conservation of valuable tracts of land.

The table below gives you a few ideas on what you can buy. You may wish to share this list with your parents or other adults. Plan to write or call these companies and ask for a copy of their latest catalog.

Product	Why Buy It	Source
Butters, spreads	Obtained from sustainable crops; donations are made to conservation groups	Moonshine Trading Company P.O. Box 896 Winters, CA 95694 (916) 753-0601
Candies and cookies	All-natural and preservative-free "goodies" from rainforest sources	Cultural Survival, Inc. 215 First Street Cambridge, MA 02142 (617) 621-3818
Cashews	Grown and harvested by indigenous peoples	Ward's Pond Farm R.F.D. 3, Box 1380 Morrisville, VT 05661 (802) 888-3001
Chocolates	Uses sustainably harvested nuts such as cashews and Brazil nuts	Blue Planet Trading Company 717 Simundson Drive, #111 Point Roberts, WA 98281
Honey	Gathered from cooperative beehives in the African rainforest	Walnut Acres Penns Creek, PA 17862 (800) 433-3998
Nuts	Harvested from sustainable resources	Pueblo to People 2105 Silber Road, Suite 101-53 Houston, TX 77006 (800) 843-5257
Nuts, dried fruits and oils	Preservative-free foods from sustainable reserves	From the Rainforest 270 Lafayette Street New York, NY 10002 (800) EARTH 96
Rainforest Crunch Ice Cream	Uses sustainably harvested nuts	Ben and Jerry's Ice Cream

The items listed provide jobs and a source of livelihood for the people who live in or near the rainforest. The growing and harvesting of these items do not harm the rainforest and are a natural use of the local environment.

Read Other Books About the Rainforest

The following books can provide you with loads of additional information and fascinating facts about life in the rainforest. In these books you'll discover unusual plants and strange animals in addition to learning about the lives of people who live in and depend upon the rainforest for their daily existence. Plan to check out some of these books from your school or public library.

Asimov, Issac. *Why Are the Rain Forests Vanishing?* Milwaukee: Gareth Stevens, 1992. The plight of the world's rainforests and the threats to their survival are detailed in this fascinating book.

Baker, Jeannie. *Where the Forest Meets the Sea.* New York: Greenwillow, 1988. You will delight in the magical and inventive illustrations used to tell the story of a disappearing Australian forest.

Baker, Lucy. *Life in the Rainforests.* New York: Franklin Watts, 1990. Explore the rich variety of plant and animal life that inhabits the many layers of a tropical rainforest.

Cherry, Lynn. *The Great Kapok Tree: A Tale of the Amazon Rain Forest.* New York: Gulliver, 1990. A beautifully illustrated story of the meaning of conservation told from the perspective of the animals who inhabit a threatened ecosystem. A "must read."

Chinery, Michael. *Rainforest Animals.* New York: Random House, 1992. Some of the world's most unusual animals can be found in a tropical rainforest as well as in the pages of this fascinating book.

Cowcher, Helen. *Rain Forest.* New York: Farrar, Straus and Giroux, 1988. This book raises ecological issues through a well-told tale and wonderful illustrations.

Dorros, Arthur. *Rain Forest Secrets.* New York: Scholastic, 1990. Lots to discover, lots to investigate and lots to learn about the rainforest can be found in this delightful book.

Dunphy, Madeleine. *At Home in the Rain Forest.* New York: Hyperion, 1994. Amazing animals and equally amazing plants can be found in the pages of this fascinating book. An "easy read."

George, Jean C. *One Day in the Tropical Rain Forest.* New York: HarperCollins, 1990. The struggle over land in the Amazon rainforest is told through the eyes of a young native boy. This is a book you will read again and again.

Gibbons, Gail. *Nature's Green Umbrella.* New York: Morrow, 1991. Come and examine the mysteries and marvels of the rainforest—unusual animals, fascinating plants and an ecosystem unlike anywhere else on earth.

Goodman, Billy. *The Rain Forest.* New York: Little, Brown, 1992. The mysterious and magical world of the rainforest is revealed in the pages of this book. You'll be amazed at the discoveries you'll make.

Hare, Tony. *Rainforest Destruction.* New York: Franklin Watts, 1990. What's happening to the rainforests of the world? Why are they threatened? Why are they being eliminated? The answers to these and other questions can be found in this informative book.

Jordan, Martin, and Tanis Jordan. *Jungle Days, Jungle Nights*. New York: Kingfisher Books, 1993. What's it like to live in the jungle? What is daily life like? Here's where you'll find all the answers.

Landau, Elaine. *Tropical Rain Forests Around the World*. New York: Franklin Watts, 1991. This book will acquaint you with the variety of animal life, the diversity of plant life and the significance of the rainforest in all our lives.

Lepthien, Emilie. *The Tropical Rain Forest*. Chicago: Children's Press, 1993. A magical journey through one of the world's most incredible ecosystems awaits you in the pages of this book.

Lewis, Scott. *The Rain Forest Book*. New York: Berkley Books, 1993. There's so much to learn and appreciate about the rainforest. This book provides a lot of information about this important ecosystem.

MacDonald, Fiona. *Rain Forest*. Austin, TX: Raintree/Steck-Vaughn, 1994. A colorful and informative journey through the different layers of the rainforest. Lots of information and loads of illustrations highlight this super book.

National Wildlife Federation editors. *Rain Forests: Tropical Treasures*. Vienna, VA: National Wildlife Federation, 1991. A magnificent book! You'll want to read it many times and share it with your friends.

Pratt, Kristin. *A Walk in the Rain Forest*. Nevada City, CA: Dawn Publications, 1992. An alphabetical trip over, under and through the rainforest. Full of information, this book was written by a seventeen-year-old high school student.

Ruiz de Larramendi, Alberto. *Tropical Rain Forests of Central America*. Chicago: Children's Press, 1993. A fascinating look at three rainforest preserves in Central America. Offers an intriguing glimpse into conservation efforts in this part of the world.

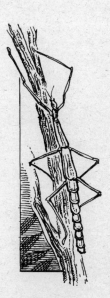

Silver, Donald. *Why Save the Rain Forest?* New York: Julian Messner, 1993. This book tells of the many dangers facing the rainforest and ways we can all work together to preserve this valuable environment.

Siy, Alexandra. *The Brazilian Rainforest*. New York: Dillon, 1992. Come and take a magical trip through one of the world's most amazing environments. You'll never know what you can discover.

Taylor, Barbara. *Rain Forest*. New York: Dorling Kindersley, 1992. A wonderfully photographed book describing some of the most unusual inhabitants of the rainforest, including a flying lizard and a poisonous frog.

Willow, Diane. *At Home in the Rain Forest*. Watertown, MA: Charlesbridge, 1991. In this book you'll take a trip from the top of the highest trees in the rainforest down through the various levels. You'll meet all sorts of unusual and strange species.

Yolen, Jane. *Welcome to the Green House*. New York: Putnam and Grosset, 1993. Rich and beautiful illustrations highlight this "journey" through the Amazonian rainforest. You'll see and hear the sounds of this incredible environment.

Purchase Recycled Paper Products

Did you know that the United States imports more than 800 million pounds of paper pulp from the Amazon each year? This paper pulp comes from trees harvested during deforestation efforts throughout the rainforest. By purchasing products made from this pulp, we are all contributing to the destruction of valuable timber. We can significantly reduce our dependency on rainforest paper pulp, however, by using recycled paper products. The following companies specialize in recycled products. Write or call them and request a current listing of their products. Be sure to share the information with your parents and friends.

Conservatree Paper Company
10 Lombard Street #250
San Francisco, CA 94111
(800) 522-9200

Recycled Products
Information Clearinghouse
(703) 941-4452

Earth Care Paper Company
P.O. Box 3335
Madison, WI 53704
(608) 256-5522

Write the Rainforest Action Network

The Rainforest Action Network is a nonprofit organization whose mission is to protect the earth's rainforests through educational programs, grassroots membership and nonviolent direct action. A major force in the preservation and conservation of valuable rainforest lands since 1985, the Network provides a wealth of outreach projects, newsletters, bulletins and public-service programs.

The Rainforest Action Network also produces a series of Fact Sheets offering updated information on the destruction and preservation of the world's rainforests. These sheets are free for the asking. Here are just a few of the dozens available:

The Clean-Up Kids (#13E)—Provides a listing of environmental groups around the country involving or started by young people just like you. This is a wonderful way to connect with students in all parts of the United States.
Native Peoples of Tropical Rainforests (#13C)—This sheet provides valuable information about the indigenous peoples of the rainforest.
Rates of Rainforest Loss (#4B)—Contains amazing information on the escalation of rainforest destruction currently taking place.

Seven Things You Can Do (#1C)—Provides seven worthwhile activities for you and your family to do right now to help preserve the rainforests of the world.

Species Extinction and the Rainforests (#3B)—Offers up-to-date information on several animal species in danger of extinction.

Tropical Rainforest Animals (#13D)—Using a question-and-answer format, this sheet offers a variety of interesting facts about the different animals of this region.

The Rainforest Action Network created the Protect-an-Acre program in 1991 to preserve the ecological and cultural integrity of the rainforest and its inhabitants. Funding is used to help indigenous people of the rainforest obtain title to their lands, to create and maintain sustainable sources of revenue and to establish property boundaries.

The money that the Network receives are used for several rainforest preservation projects. Donors to the program receive an attractive certificate of recognition along with descriptions of funded projects. This is an excellent opportunity for you, your family or your class to make an important contribution in preserving the world's rainforests.

Write or call the Rainforest Action Network at 450 Sansome Street, Suite 700, San Francisco, CA 94111, (415) 398-4404 and ask for their current listing of available Fact Sheets. Be sure to share these sheets with your parents and teacher.

Backyard Wildlife Habitat Program

Many families and many kids around the country are actively participating in environmental issues through a unique program administered by the National Wildlife Federation. This program—the Backyard Wildlife Habitat Program—allows families to turn some or all of their backyard into an official habitat for various animals. The NWF provides families with instructions and detailed information on how they can establish and maintain a functioning wildlife preserve in their backyard. After a family has set up its yard, family members can send their plan and $5.00 to the NWF. The NWF will look it over, make recommendations, and certify the area as an official Backyard Wildlife Habitat.

If you or your family is interested in participating in this program, write for more information to National Wildlife Federation (Backyard Wildlife Habitat Program, 1400 16th Street NW, Washington, DC 20036).

Adopt an Endangered Animal

Write to the American Association of Zoological Parks and Aquariums (4550 Montgomery Avenue, Suite 940N, Bethesda, MD 20814). Ask about information on "adopting" an endangered animal. For a fee you (or you and your family) can "adopt" an animal and provide resources that will help in preserving that specific individual as well as members of that species.

Plant Some Trees

By planting trees you are helping contribute to the world's oxygen supply. Approximately 50 percent of the world's oxygen comes from the rainforest. By planting and caring for trees in your local community, you are helping reduce the carbon dioxide in the air while adding beauty to the environment. Here are some organizations that can help you in your tree-planting efforts: National Arbor Day Foundation (Arbor Lodge 100, Nebraska City, NE 68410), American Forestry Association (Global ReLeaf Program, P.O. Box 2000, Washington, DC 20013) and Tree People (12601 Mulholland Drive, Beverly Hills, CA 90210).

Rainforest Awareness Week

Write to Creating Our Future (398 North Ferndale, Mill Valley, CA 94941) and ask for a copy of *How to Organize a Rainforest Awareness Week at Your School*. This publication describes a program developed and organized by a group of high school students. Be sure to share it with your teacher.

Fascinating Facts

Fascinating Facts About Rainforests

Although rainforests cover only about 6 percent of the earth's surface, they are home to more than 50 percent of the plant and animal species in the world.

Rainforests are the most complex ecosystems in the world and contain an abundant reserve of resources.

Tropical rainforests play an important role in regulating the world's climate through their position in the oxygen, carbon and water cycles.

The largest rainforest in the world is located in South America; the smallest rainforest is in Australia.

Believe it or not—parts of western Canada and southeast Alaska have rainforests.

Antarctica and Europe are the only continents that do not have rainforests.

Every year the world loses an area of tropical rainforest nearly as large as the state of Washington.

Tropical rainforests may get up to 400 inches of rain each year—that's more than 33 feet of water!

In one year, the rainforest in Cherrapunji, India, got 1,042 inches of rain, more than 20 times the annual rainfall of New York City.

Much of India's rainforests have been successfully converted to national parks.

Two hundred years ago rainforests covered 14 percent of all the land in the world; today they cover about 6 percent.

People are working to save the rainforests by passing international laws that limit destruction and by offering financial help to countries to persuade them to stop cutting down trees.

Approximately 50 percent of all the earth's oxygen comes from the rainforest.

The Amazon rainforest is the largest in the world; it covers 2.3 million square miles and extends over nine South American countries.

The difference between the hottest and coldest months in the rainforest is less than 10°F.

Many scientists consider the rainforests of the world as the most important source for new medicines, particularly drugs used in the fight against cancer.

The United States has a tropical rainforest on the islands of Hawaii.

Fascinating Facts About Rainforest Animals

The curly-haired tarantula can capture and eat small birds.

There are more than 235 kinds of hummingbirds and 150 types of butterflies in the tropical rainforests of South America.

One million termites can rid the rainforest of over 10 tons of wood within a year.

Army ants will often travel in groups of up to 20 million strong. They will destroy and eat everything in their path.

The Goliath beetle grows up to 6 inches long and sounds like a small aircraft when it flies.

The basilisk lizard can run across the top of water.

The African giant snail grows up to 15 inches long.

The anaconda, the world's largest snake, can grow to over 30 feet in length and weigh up to 330 pounds.

The flying snake can glide through the air from tree to tree.

One variety of the poison dart frog has enough poison in its skin to kill six people.

The bill of a toucan bird is made of keratin, the same material in your fingernails.

The flying gecko, a rainforest lizard, has flaps of skin along its sides that act like a parachute—allowing it to glide through the air from tree to tree.

Tiger centipedes can have as many as 23 pairs of legs.

Twenty percent of all bird species are found in the rainforests of the Amazon.

Sticky suckers on the feet of tree frogs allow them to cling upside down on branches for many hours.

Before it changes into a butterfly, the postman caterpillar will eat 25,000 times its own weight in flower leaves.

The world's largest eagle—the harpy eagle—grows to a height of 3 feet.

The ruby topaz hummingbird beats its wings at the rate of 50 times every second.

The fur of a sloth is green because of all the algae that grows on it.

Some bats can catch more than 600 insects in one hour.

Fascinating Facts About Rainforest Plants

Tropical forests contain 155,000 of the 250,000 known plant species in the world.

The largest flower in the world—the rafflesia—is 3 feet across and weighs 36 pounds.

More than 1,500 different varieties of vegetables can be found in the rainforests of the world.

More than 500 different types of trees and 1,500 different flowering plants may grow on 1 acre of rainforest land.

About 25 percent of all the medicines used in the world come from the plants of the rainforest.

At least 1,400 rainforest plants are known to offer cures for various forms of cancer.

About 10,000 varieties of trees can be found in the rainforests of Indonesia.

There are more than 20,000 different types of orchids growing in a tropical rainforest.

Several orchids in the rainforest have a small ledge that serves as a "landing pad" for flying insects.

When trees are cut down, tropical rains will wash away 450 tons of fertile topsoil from a single acre of land.

Some rainforest plants have chemical poisons to kill the insects that feed on them.

Approximately 80 percent of all surface vegetation is in the rainforest.

Only 1 percent of all the rainforest plants have been screened for medical use. That means that the cure for dangerous and deadly diseases may be found someday in the remaining 99 percent of the plants in the rainforest.

Glossary

Biodiversity: This is the condition of a community of living things that occurs when there is a wide variety of plant and animal life.

Biome: An area of land or ocean that contains specific types of plants and/or animals. It may also have a particular kind of weather.

Bromeliads: Members of the pineapple family that live on the surface of other plants (see **Epiphyte**).

Buttresses: Supporting structures that grow from the base of a tree's trunk and help support the weight of that tree.

Camouflage: The shape or color of an organism that helps it hide from its enemies.

Canopy: The third layer of the rainforest—between the understory layer and the emergent layer. This part of the rainforest typically has the most plant and animal life.

Climate: The type of weather that is normally expected in an area of the world over a long period of time (years, for example). In general, we expect that the tropics will be hot and wet and that the arctic regions will be cold.

Decomposers: Organisms that feed on the dead bodies of other organisms. This feeding process helps break down dead and decaying material.

Deforestation: The large-scale destruction of parts of the rainforest through cutting and/or burning of trees.

Diversity: A wide variety of items (plants or animals, for example).

Ecology: The relationship between plants and animals (including humans) and their environment.

Environment: Places and conditions in which plants and animals (and perhaps humans) live together.

Emergent layer: This is the top layer of the rainforest containing the tops of trees—many reaching heights of 250 feet or more.

Epiphyte: A plant that grows on another plant. Rainforest epiphytes obtain all their nutrients and water high above the forest floor.

Equator: An imaginary line around the earth, it divides the earth into two halves—the Northern and Southern Hemispheres.

Erosion: The washing away of soil through the action of running water or blowing wind.

Evapotranspiration: A natural process in which water from many plants evaporates throughout the rainforest, forming a dense layer of water vapor and high levels of humidity.

Extinct: When a plant or animal species is wiped out—and no longer exists.

Global warming: A condition in which portions of the world heat up to temperatures not normally expected. The burning of large portions of the rainforest contributes to global warming.

Greenhouse effect: The warming of the lower atmosphere that occurs when large amounts of carbon dioxide gas trap heat that would normally escape into the atmosphere.

Humus: Soil composed of dead or decaying plant and animal life. This may consist of leaf matter, plants, insects, small animals and so on.

Interdependence: The idea that everything in nature is connected to everything else; what happens to one plant or animal also affects other plants and animals.

Liana: A specific type of woody vine that grows up the trunk of a tree, usually at a very rapid rate.

Litter: Dead plant life such as leaves, twigs and branches that accumulate on the forest floor.

Logging: The cutting and removal of trees for use as lumber.

Nutrients: The food materials needed by plants and animals to survive.

Predator: Any animal that survives by killing and eating other animals; for example, snakes, frogs and jaguars.

Producers: Plants that are able to make their own food.

Slash-and-burn agriculture: A type of farming in which people cut down large stands of trees and burn the debris. The cleared land is then used for farming or ranching.

Species: A group of plants or animals able to produce new plants or animals that carry some of the characteristics of the parents.

Species diversity: The variety of plant and/or animal species that inhabit a specific area.

Sustainable development: The harvesting and use of rainforest products in a way that preserves the balance of nature without adversely affecting the environment.

Topsoil: The surface layer of dirt in which plants grow. Typically, it is the most nutrient-rich part of the ground.

Transpiration: The loss of water through the surfaces of a plant.

Tropical rainforest: A series of evergreen forests forming a "belt" around the equator. Typically found between the Tropic of Cancer and the Tropic of Capricorn, these areas are characterized by dense foliage, a diversity of animal life and high rainfall.

Understory layer: The second layer of a tropical rainforest. Short plants and limited sunlight are characteristic of this area.

Weather: The atmospheric conditions that happen in an area during a specific and short period of time, such as a few hours or a few days.

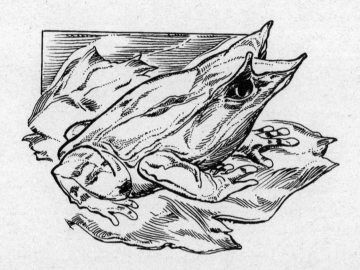

Index

E

Earthworms, 32, 33
Ecologically diverse, 36
Ecosystem, vi, 3, 79, 80, 82
Ecotourism Society, 90
Ecotourism, 90
Elodia plants, 80
Emergent trees, 65, 66, 68
Emergent layer, 65
Endangered species, 57
Environment
    ideal, 36
    in danger, v
    local, 6, 7
    self-sufficient, 3
Environmental Groups
    Children's Alliance for Protection
      of the Environment, 93
    Children's Rainforest, 94
    Conservation International, 94
    Cultural Survival, 94
    Defenders of Wildlife, 94
    Friends of the Earth, 94
    Friends of Wildlife Conservation,
      94
    Marine World Africa USA, 94
    National Audubon Society, 94
    National Wildlife Federation, 94
    Natural Resources Defense Council,
      94
    Nature Conservancy International,
      94
    Rainforest Action Network, 94
    Rainforest Alliance, 94
    Rainforest Preservation Founda-
      tion, 95
    Save the Rainforest, 95
    Sierra Club, 95
    Smithsonian Tropical Research
      Institute, 95

Tree Amigos/Center for Environ-
  mental Study, 95
Trees for the Future, 95
The Wilderness Society, 95
World-Wide Fund for Nature, 95
Epiphytes, 60
Equator, 9
Erosion, 86
Ethnobotony, 78
Extinction, 57
Extractive reserves, 88

F

Fact sheets, 100
Fascinating facts
    about rainforests, 103
    about rainforest animals, 104
    about rainforest plants, 105
Field notes, 6
Flora and fauna, 82
Food
    banana, 76
    chocolate, 76
    coffee, 76
    grapefruit, 76
    pineapples, 76
    oranges, 76
    sugar, 76
    tea, 76
    tomato, 76
Food web, 12
Food chain, 11
Forest floor, 23
Frogs, 36
Fungi, 30

G

Government officials, 95
Grass, 86, 87
Greenhouse effect, 76

If you enjoyed
Exploring the Rainforest,
you won't want to miss these exciting books!

Max Bonker and the Howling Thieves

Scott Weidensaul and Bruce Van Patter
Illustrated by Bruce Van Patter
Join Max Bonker, detective extraordinaire, as he outwits the evil Rathbone and solves an Amazon rainforest mystery.

Ages 6 and up.
ISBN 1-55591-244-3, 8 $^1/_2$ x 11
32 pages, hardcover
$16.95

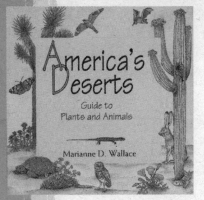

America's Deserts

Guide to Plants and Animals
Marianne D. Wallace

Explore one of the most fascinating ecosystems with this detailed guide to the plants and animals of the Chihuahuan, Great Basin, Sonoran and Mojave deserts.

Ages 8 and up.
ISBN 1-55591-268-0, 9 x 9
48 pages, paperback
$15.95

Eco-Women

Protectors of the Earth
Willow Ann Sirch

Meet Jane Goodall, Rachel Carson and seven other important women and organizations who have made vital contributions to our environment.

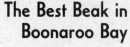

Ages 8 and up.
ISBN 1-55591-252-4, 7 x 9
96 pages, paperback
$15.95

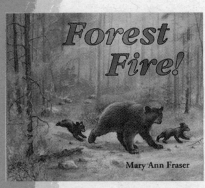

Forest Fire!

Mary Ann Fraser

Learn how a forest fire transforms the environment and how the surviving plants and animals thrive again.

Ages 5 and up.
ISBN 1-55591-251-6, 10 x 8 $^1/_2$
32 pages, hardcover
$17.95

The Best Beak in Boonaroo Bay

Narelle Oliver

Discover how the quarreling birds decide who has the best beak in the Australian mangrove swamp.

Ages 5 and up.
ISBN 1-55591-227-3, 8 $^1/_2$ x 11
32 pages, hardcover
$15.95